Cats
in the
Parsonage

CLAIR SHAFFER, JR.

Evergreen
PRESS

ISBN 1-58169-060-6
For Worldwide Distribution
Printed in the U.S.A.

Evergreen Press
P.O. Box 91011 • Mobile, AL 36691

Table of Contents

ACKNOWLEDGMENTS

First and foremost, I am thankful to God the Father and the Lord Jesus Christ who sought me and saved me, and delivered me from a meaningless life and a horrible eternity. My thanks to the Holy Spirit who seeks to guide me and empower me each day of my life.

Thank you to my beautiful and wonderful wife, the co-author of this book, who remembered many details, corrected me on my recollections of incidents, read or listened to what I wrote, and encouraged me when I lagged in completing this project.

Many thanks to Gail Martz who painstakingly typed the manuscript while trying to read my sometimes jumbled printing. Gail also types the outlines for my messages that are placed in the Sunday bulletins of both our churches. I could never repay her fully for all she has done for me. She is to be commended for her dedication to the Lord and His work.

I want to express my gratitude to all the members and friends of St. Elias and Zion Reformed Churches. There are many who have gone on to be with the Lord since we came here in 1984. I have not and will not forget them. Our people have been a great inspiration and an encouragement to Brenda and me all through the years. They have stood behind us and have helped us in so many ways. I appreciate each one of them and love them dearly in the Lord.

I also want to thank the many friends who have been an inspiration to me in the writing of this book. My attorney, Bob Diehl, who encouraged me to write about a popular subject but to also share my faith in Jesus Christ; to Foster Furman who also encouraged me with his "Stick-to-itiveness" philosophy and strong spirituality; to the fine people at the Sunbury Animal Hospital who provided much information about the two felines in my house; to Thelma Deroba, a member of our Zion Church and an animal lover, cats especially, who has lovingly encouraged me to go for my dream; to Barb Bolig, a dear friend and cat lover whose advice has helped immensely in raising our two furballs; and of course, to Taffy and Tiffany without whom this book would not be possible.

Brenda and I are not the only "cat lovers" in our charge. Taffy and Tiffany have several counterparts whom we have had the privilege to meet. I wish to recognize these feline friends as being part of our "family."

Other Parish Pussycats:

"TOMMY" Aumiller
"TIGGER" Deroba
"SONNY" Einsig
"PUDGE" Heim
"CINNAMON" Kemberling
"FEATHER" Leppert
"STOSH" Messner

Our apologies to any we have missed.

DEDICATION

To my parents, Clair and Louella Shaffer,
who gave me the right tools with which to build a life.
May God bless them abundantly.

INTRODUCTION

This is a book about cats and two felines in particular, Taffy and Tiffany, known affectionately as the "parsonage cats." It may be a book about my philosophy of life as well since I cannot help but share my faith in and appreciation to the Lord. So bear with me in my new adventure as I seek to entertain you and also perhaps influence you to give your life to God if you have not already done so.

I love animals, cats and dogs especially, but I am not an animal activist. I find "activism" to be an extreme, and I truly feel that extremes tend to isolate individuals from ordinary people and give the impression of being odd or eccentric. However, I am definitely opposed to animal cruelty and find such treatment inexcusable for any reason, experimentation included. Proverbs 12:10 states, "An upright person sees to the needs of his animal, but the kindest acts of the callous are cruel." It is man's God-given responsibility to care for animals, wild and domestic, and to intelligently live in harmony with them. They are here for our use (see Genesis 4:2,3;10:9) and enjoyment (see 2 Samuel 12:1-4), and we can become very attached to them. For many of us animal lovers, they are like family.

And so I hope you enjoy this true story of two little cats, set down in simple, everyday language and basically written in a chronological order of events. Brenda and I have thoroughly enjoyed being "owned" by our little companions over the years and have tried to honor their natural inbred independence as much as possible.

Clair F. Shaffer Jr.

Chapter 1

Candy, the Original Parsonage Cat

Some years before we moved into the parsonage, a little gray and white striped tiger cat showed up in the neighborhood. She became known as Candy and adopted our neighbors as her own extended family. She was a friendly feline and traveled from house to house for handouts as well as catching mice, squirrels, chipmunks, and a variety of birds. This tough little scrapper once even had a groundhog cornered and was ready to take it on until Jim, our neighbor's son, intervened and took care of the intruder.

Candy also backed down a Rottweiler, many times her size, which had appeared in the neighborhood one summer day. This big puppy had a collar but no identification and seemed friendly enough; yet, we were concerned having him around since we knew nothing about him. He had treed Candy's kittens in the magnolia and was coming down through our backyard when he spotted Candy slowly walking from our porch up towards Louise's garden. He came charging at her at full gallop barking loudly. Candy stopped with one front paw slightly raised, her head turned toward her would-be attacker, looking like a pointer. When Candy did not run or even flinch, the dog slowed his pace and came to a halt. Candy did not move, did not make a sound, did not even bristle up one hair. She simply stood her ground in the same position and stared at the now not-so-sure-of himself doggie. This went on for a short time, and finally the Rottweiler whined pathetically, backed up, and ran behind my car parked in the driveway. Candy then resumed her trek up through the lawn slowly taking her time. Brenda and I watched this episode in amazement and thought to ourselves, *What a cool cat.*

Ardis, one of our parishioners, offered this neat analysis: "If Candy could have talked she would have said, 'OK, Mutt...make my day!'" We echo a hearty amen! And yes, there was a happy ending for the dog. Calls to the state police and the dog catcher proved futile, but thankfully his owner came looking for him later in the day. Blue, as he was called, was very happy to see his master. Until she arrived, Blue went to a spot near the garage and kept a wary eye out for "Dirty" Candy. It seems that he had a habit of taking off from the farm his master owned up the valley near our home. If no one was around, Blue went looking for companionship. We just happened to be the lucky ones this time.

Candy became known as "The Parsonage Cat" because she spent a lot of time in the house playing with the former minister's children. One of our regular members, Bob Radel, actually coined the name and kiddingly told us when my wife Brenda and I moved in that now Candy was our cat. There was a lot of truth in that because it didn't take long for us to become very fond of Candy, and we enjoyed caring for her with love, food, and some medicine.

She had her first litter shortly afterwards, and we were blessed with five little kittens that Candy was more than willing to share with us. Brenda had fun naming them, all females, as follows: Smokey, Tyco, Charcoal, Coco, and Tigger. Smokey, a black cat with some gold spattering throughout and a beige spot on her right front foot, was Brenda's favorite.

Smokey made many trips into the parsonage, usually to see me in my study. Brenda would plop her down in the middle of my desk, and Smokey would promptly remove the pens from my pocket. She was quite adept at it, using her front paws or her teeth. She then pushed them around on my desk and off the edge if I let her. We often talked about bringing her inside permanently but never got around to it.

We enjoyed watching the kittens grow; and as we showered them with attention, they claimed our back porch as their home. Each night they would curl up beside the trash can against the back of the house all huddled together. In the morning, Candy would usually be gone when we opened the door, and the kittens would hurry to greet us. We fed them dried cat food after they were old enough to eat it, and they dug into it like there was no tomorrow. They were equally eager when their mom nursed them, and they seemed to have their own favorite feeding spot on her belly. Candy brought them other "food" as well.

I remember Brenda's reaction one day as she was watching the kittens out the back door. She yelled to me in the kitchen, "Clair! Candy has a mouse."

"Is it dead or alive?"

"I'm not sure…I think it's dead."

"Which one is she giving it to?"

"Smokey!"

"YUK!" I laughed out loud.

"I'm glad you think it's funny."

"It's all part of their learning process," I protested. "She will do this for each one of them."

"What's the next step in the process?" Brenda wanted to know.

"Live ones…for them to kill."

"Gross!"

I laugh again, getting a kick out of my city girl's exposure to more country life. And sure enough, there was a parade of mice, ground moles, and chipmunks for these little some day hunters to practice on. It amazed Brenda how Candy would single out the kitten to which she gave the prey and then keep the others away. I explained that they all had to learn and that Candy would see to it that each one did. The cat is a very intelligent animal, and despite some early beliefs to the contrary, its brain is the closest in shape to a human's of all the animals. It is just fascinating to watch them work and overcome obstacles and problems. I believe that animals do "reason" to a certain extent. Have you ever noticed how a cat will sit and watch you for an extended period of time? It's eerie!

Besides being very intelligent, cats are extremely playful. We thoroughly enjoyed watching our new little tenants go through their cute playtime routines. As they grew, it became evident that Smokey was the biggest and strongest of the kittens, Coco was next, then Charcoal, and Tyco was the runt. By this time, Tigger had been adopted by a family nearby.

Smokey seemed to have perfected the art of lying on her back and grabbing one of her sisters by the head with her front feet and clobbering it with her back feet. Needless to say, once released they would stagger away like a dazed pugilist. We observed all the kittens using this maneuver but not as often as or as well as Miss Smokey.

Brenda's favorite little feline had another cute but not-so-commendable habit. Smokey loved the element of surprise—she loved to pounce on her unsuspecting sisters. However, she did not always succeed. More often than not, she would miss her intended prey and slam into some inanimate object. The first time we saw her do this, she hit the garbage can. The next time, it was our metal storm door. Then one day we were relaxing on the back porch and heard a loud "thud" around the corner of the house by the driveway. Smokey had attempted one of her patented leaps and crashed headfirst into the side of the house. Now aluminum siding gives to a certain degree, but it was not made for kitty cats to bounce their heads on. We laughed when Smokey came staggering around the corner looking like a drunken sailor.

Charcoal, almost Smokey's twin, was an adorable little squirt who would leap upon your back if you knelt down. She was careful, it seemed, not to extend her claws unless it was cold and we had heavy coats on. Once up on our backs, she would nuzzle and purr and lick our hair, ears, etc. She was a friendly cat who followed us around and would spend hours in our company. If I worked in my wood shop, Charcoal would come in with me and after making a nuisance of herself, would lie down in some cozy spot, watch for a while, and usually take a nap. It seemed she did this about every Saturday that I worked in the shop. She didn't seem to mind the noise of the tools or all the dust my wood projects created.

Coco was an orange, black, and white calico. She was sleek and beautiful but didn't seem to mind getting dirty—in fact, downright filthy. Cats normally do not like to get wet, but Coco would go wading through the stream across the road from the parsonage. One day she showed up on the back porch absolutely filthy, covered with something like black grease and smelling terrible. Brenda and our neighbor girls, Jen and Jo, put her in a bucket and washed her with dish detergent. At first, Coco squirmed a bit but then accepted the inevitable. After her ordeal, she went aside and improved upon the girls' job. She was quite the little groomer and would spend hours, so it seemed, prettying herself up. She, too, was a friendly and loving cat.

Tyco—ah yes, Tyco! I saved telling about Tyco for last, first of all because she would become the mother of our official inside "Parsonage Cats" and secondly, because of her tenacity and courage. I will share more about this remarkable cat in the next chapter concerning her exploits as a mother, midwife, and nurse. At this point, I wish to talk about her personality and how she compensated for being the runt of the litter by becoming the most aggressive one. This behavior began at feeding times on the back porch. It was quite a scene to watch as this small kitten made the others wait to eat until she was finished. Tyco's strategy was simple: scare the daylights out of her rivals by a swipe to the head and by hissing and growling. It was effective, and she gained the respect (or fear) of Smokey, Charcoal, and Coco.

Later on, an Angora cat named Fluffy (or Puffy as Jen and Jo called her) joined our little crew out back. She was one of the "barn cats" from our neighbor Bill's farm next door. Apparently Fluffy wandered over the road from the barn and decided to take up residence with the cats on our porch. She was a feisty little thing for her size but was no match for Tyco, who quickly put her in her place. This tiger-calico (hence her name "Tyco") even tried to back down her mother Candy who would tolerate her antics to a certain degree, but then with one swipe of her paw would send Tyco rolling across the cement.

I attempted to discipline Tyco with a few "swipes" of my own across her backside plus a few other tactics, but it was to no avail. She was a strong-willed and determined little pussycat. I decided it was just the "Law of the Jungle" and tried to feed Tyco separately from the others. This worked much better, and the rest of the crew seemed happy with the arrangement.

A New Dwelling Place

As fall grew near, I became increasingly concerned about the kittens on the back porch. My first provision of shelter for them had been a cardboard box with the rug and sweatshirts inside. The kittens seemed to sense it was for them and took to it right away. Before long, however, cold weather would be setting in, and I felt they needed more than that to keep them warm. Inclement weather made it evident that the cardboard box would not be substantial enough. I had to come up with another idea.

The garage at the parsonage serves also as my wood shop.

Some of our parishioners were surprised that we could park both cars in the building and I would still have room to work. It's much larger than it looks. It measures 20 feet, 7 inches wide by 24 feet, 5 inches long. When we moved there, the garage did not look too healthy. Martin Raker, our Joint Consistory President at the time, suggested putting a chain around it and pulling it down. After much discussion, it was decided that fixing it up would be the least expensive action because a new building would simply cost too much. One of the men from our Zion Church, Richard Meiser, was hired to repair the garage, and I assisted him.

During this time I decided to build the kittens a house. Our neighbor, Louise, cautioned us not to call it a "cat house," and we readily agreed. It certainly would not do for a minister and his wife to have a cat house out back. We settled on the title, "a house for the cats." I used quarter-inch plywood and some pine braces to construct the house with a roof that could be lifted off it so that we could easily inspect and clean it. I cut out a six by six inch doorway, but decided that windows were not necessary since we were more concerned with the cats' warmth and comfort.

My daughters Karena and Kamielle were up from Lancaster staying with us this particular weekend, and we all became involved in the project. We had some old carpet that we used to insulate the house and make a nice bedding for our five tenants who inspected their new quarters and moved right in. It seemed to give them a better sense of security than the flimsy box, and when it thundered and stormed, they ran into their shelter and huddled together. The house measured 30" long, 16" wide, and 19" high at the peak of the roof. There seemed to be ample room for all five of them, and they got along well together. Candy did not join them in the house after they were bigger, although she did stop by to visit them often.

The kittens even came up with a sleeping arrangement. Tyco, Smokey, Coco, and Charcoal took either one of the three sides or the middle of the house as their sleeping spots. Fluffy, who was no relation to the four sisters, was forced to sleep in the doorway. When we peeked out the window at the house, we would see Fluffy's bushy tail protruding out the doorway. There never seemed to be any change in this arrangement. It appeared to be an order they decided upon and stuck to.

As the year came to a close, we lost two of our five furry friends to one of cat's most formidable enemies—the automobile. Smokey was the first victim. We had gone away for the weekend and when we returned home, we saw her lying by the side of the road where we turn into our driveway. It had snowed quite a bit, and the plows piled it high along the highway. It looked as if Smokey may have become trapped between the car and the snow and panicked. We retrieved her frozen-stiff body and took it to the back porch where we ceremoniously displayed it to the other cats and warned them that the same thing would happen to them if they did not stay off the road. They wanted nothing to do with Smokey's dead body; apparently, the presence of death repulsed them. I told Brenda that our efforts to teach them would be futile and that they would not listen to our pleas.

It was soon obvious that I was unfortunately right because about a month or so later, Charcoal was hit by a car and was crying in pain. Our neighbor, Louise, found her and diagnosed a broken back and other injuries. Louise called Bill, who mercifully put her to sleep. Now we had three pussycats left, and we wondered how long they would last with their stubborn tendency to cross the roads.

It is a tough world out there, as our cats found out. The Lord promised that "While you are in this world, you are going to have trouble" (John 16:33). We are to expect to have some trouble, even if we are doing the right thing. The answer is not to try and run from it. Difficulties do not usually just go away when we want them to. They must be faced and dealt with; this is where our faith in God comes in. He helps us face and deal with adversity and find creative solutions.

We must give God the chance to to do something great with our lives. We don't have to be down and out before we turn to Him to find what is missing in our life. Even successful, wealthy, and influential people have found that there is an emptiness inside of them that cries out for fulfillment. That's because God has created us to communicate with Him and have a relationship with Him that only He can fill.

We, as people living on God's good green earth, may not always know exactly what our Creator is doing in our lives at a given time. I know the cats sometimes can't quite figure us out, but just as they accepted their new house without much ado, we need to trust our Father with what He provides us. We can become completely confident that He has our best interests at heart. "Since God is for us, who can be against us?" (Romans 8:31)

Chapter 2

Taffy and Tiffany Are Born

The winter season was coming to a close, and we were all looking forward to spring. The older I get, the more I do not care for cold weather and all that goes with it. Snow, ice, sub-degree temperatures, drab colors, etc., do not appeal to me. Even autumn is not quite so enjoyable for me any longer; it only reminds me of what is coming next. I yearn for the warmth and the bright colors of spring and summer.

Tyco, Coco, and Fluffy were still sharing the house on the back porch. All three were "with child." Tyco was the first to deliver, and at this point in time, she no longer wanted to share the house. The feisty little feline claimed it for her little family and expelled Coco and Fluffy in no uncertain terms. We heard hissing and growling sounds emanating from the porch as Tyco aggressively defended what she thought was her territory. After a short time, the other two cats complied without protest and did not attempt to enter the house.

Soon, Easter came and things changed. It was time for Fluffy to deliver her kittens. A strange occurrence took place. Tyco must have repented of her former attitude, for she completely changed and allowed Fluffy to enter their house.

Tyco, the Midwife

As I mentioned previously, Fluffy was an Angora with long beige fur. If soaking wet, she did not look much bigger than a rat. After Tyco allowed her in the house, Fluffy went into labor and tried to deliver her litter. She became weak and was having trouble bringing forth her kittens. What happened next was nothing less than incredible. Tyco got up from her own kittens and went over to help Fluffy. Brenda had gone out to check on Tyco and her brood and lifted the roof off the house. I was on the phone when I heard her urgent cry. After excusing myself, I ran out back to see what all the fuss was about. I could hardly believe my eyes! There in the house Tyco was delivering Fluffy's kittens. She pulled the little ones out—there were just two—chewed off the cords, cleaned up the afterbirth (as cats do), then proceeded to wash both newborns as well as Fluffy. She next maneuvered the kittens into position and nursed them herself. Tyco did this for about a week because Fluffy was too weak to nurse these hungry little critters. Brenda and I placed food and water right next to Fluffy in the house, and she seemed very happy.

About 45 minutes after Tyco finished her first midwife duties, Brenda went out to check on our new additions and yelled excitedly for me once again. She had taken the roof off and lo and behold, Coco was now delivering her litter. Tyco was performing her midwife duties once again and repeating all she had done for Fluffy. Everything seemed to be going well as the first two kittens were born, but then the third one became a problem—it was breach. Then little Tyco went to work. She pulled, she pushed, she twisted, and she delivered the third and final kitten. Again she cleaned everything up, nursed the newborns, and made sure Fluffy and Coco were both comfortable and that their kittens were with them. Brenda and I checked to be certain that all three mothers had their own food and water, especially Fluffy and Coco, who were quite weak after their ordeal.

Kitty "Kooperation"

It was amazing to us to see the change in Tyco after all three of the cats had their kittens. A spirit of cooperation emerged among the mothers, and when Fluffy and Coco were stronger, they nursed each other's babies. At first we had nine kittens, but two died: one of Fluffy's, which was laying outside the house one morning; and Coco's breach kitten, which Brenda found under the pile of the little ones in the house. We disposed of the dead kittens and kept a close eye on the progress of the others.

God's wonders and mysteries never cease to amaze me. Brenda and I often talk of Tyco's heroics and are convinced that we witnessed much more than pure instinct. Sure, animals are endowed with God-given instincts which guide and prompt them to act in certain ways. Many accounts have been reported of animals adopting another's offspring, even those of another species. However, I have never personally heard of an animal delivering the litter of another, whether it was the same species or not. It may have happened—I am not saying it hasn't. Brenda and I just thank the Lord that He allowed us to see one of the marvelous wonders of His creation.

The three mothers continued to get along very well. They nursed and cared for each other's kittens, shared hunting duties, and even ate in shifts. Tyco acted like a changed cat, abandoning her "bully" tactics. She couldn't do enough for Fluffy and Coco and their little ones. I told Brenda that it was the result of her living with a pastor and his wife. Our influence had made a difference in her life, and Tyco became a "spiritually" minded pussycat. Brenda's reply to my claim was, "Yeah...right!"

An amusing incident took place one morning while Tyco was minding the store. Coco and Fluffy had gone foraging, and our little heroine was tending to the flock. Brenda went out on the back porch, and Tyco came out of the house to greet her. Seeing that the other two mothers were not present, Brenda decided to give Tyco a special treat. She placed some soft cat food in front of Tyco who promptly turned and went back into the house. Brenda was puzzled for a moment until Tyco returned and plopped a freshly-killed mouse at her feet. It was her "special treat" for her friend who had been so kind in caring for her. I am sure that Tyco fully expected Brenda to eat the mouse. She sat there, looked up at Brenda, looked at the mouse, and waited. Needless to say, my usually accommodating wife did not consume her special treat, but tried her best to express her gratitude to Tyco and explain why she couldn't eat the mouse. I don't think Tyco fully understood what Brenda was trying to tell her, but later on she took the deceased rodent back into the house and made a meal of him. There didn't seem to be any hurt feelings, but Tyco didn't offer us any more treats. Once, however, when I was up near the garage, Tyco came over to me and proudly dropped a live chipmunk on the driveway. The poor little guy seemed to sense his doom, and he ran between my feet as if hoping I would rescue him. I stepped aside and told him, "Sorry, old chap...she would just catch you again. I'm not going to interfere." After toying with her prey for a while, I saw her enjoying chipmunk-a-la-lawn.

There are different theories as to why cats bring their owners mice and other kills. The one I first heard and probably the most popular among cat lovers is that they want to show off the prize of their hunt. Tyco certainly seemed very proud of the mouse and the chipmunk. However, I feel the second theory I read about is better and makes more sense: the cat is bringing its owner, or the person it has adopted, some food. Through many years of research and observation, animal experts now believe that the cat is bringing food to its human much like it does to its kittens. I am also convinced that it is a way for the cat to express love for its human—love, that is, from a feline point of view. We know that they show affection, and despite their independence, they want to be with people. Of course, like people, cats are different, and they vary in their desire for affection and company.

Watching the New Kittens Grow

Time passes very quickly, and we watched as the little fur-balls grew from tiny moist creatures into scampering, cute kittens. We tried not to interfere too much for fear that the mothers might move them, but actually it seemed that they liked us to be there and make a fuss over both mothers and kittens. Neither Tyco, Coco, nor Fluffy showed any concern when we held their little ones. I guess they trusted us and sensed that we would not harm them. We felt like babysitters when all three would go hunting or possibly just take a break and leave us with the kittens. It was fun to watch them play and grow as the days went on.

After four weeks had passed, we were sitting on the back porch one day and began to come up with names for each of the little ones. We started with Tyco's brood, of which there were four. These little darlings consisted of two calicos, a gray and white female, and one all gray male. One of the calicos was gold, black, and white and the other was gray, white, and beige. I learned something here. I had always thought that a calico cat was gold, black, and white. I was surprised to learn that any female cat that is three or more colors is a calico.

I told Brenda to do the honors of assigning names to the kittens. She named the gold, black, and white calico, "Calie." The all gray male became "Pewter." She had some trouble with naming the gray, white, and beige kitten, so I picked it up and said, "She looks like a little piece of taffy." Brenda liked it and it stuck. Taffy's gray and white colors made the beige appear to be pink. I was reminded of the taffy candy bars my parents sold in their grocery store in the fifties and early sixties—some were chocolate, some were vanilla, some strawberry, and some banana. Then there were mixed flavors, and it was one of these that came to mind as I looked at Taffy.

I handed the newly dubbed furball to Brenda and with a gleam in her eye, she asked, "Can I take her in?"

I replied, "You mean inside?"

"Yes."

"Inside the house?"

"Yes!"

"This house?" (Pointing to the parsonage.)

"Yeah!" (with a little determination)

"Well-llll...I don't know...we live here but we don't own the house...I'm not sure."

"Please?" (batting her pretty baby browns...)

"I'll check with the Consistory. We'll see what they say to our having an inside pet."

"OK!" (seeming assured the answer would be yes...)

"I have a suggestion...if it's all right with the Consistory."

"What's that?" (with baby browns questioning me...)

"We should bring in two of them to keep each other company, you know, when we're not here."

"OK! Sounds good to me."

I went on to explain to Brenda how I wished I had also bought Tiffany's (a Siamese that I once owned) sister. At the time, I was involved with both work and school, and I had to be away from my apartment quite a bit. Looking back on the experience, I felt it probably had not been good for my cat to be alone so much. Tiffany always loved to be with me, and I know she got lonely waiting for me to come home. If we were able to take a cat into the house as a pet, we both agreed we should take two. (By the way, it was approved.)

"But which one?" Brenda asked, looking the other kittens over.

"Not the male," I said, "It should be one of the other females."

"How about this little cutie?" I asked as I picked up the gray and white female.

"She is cute. What will we name her?"

"I have no idea…what do you suggest?

"How about Tiffany? Tiffany II after my Siamese."

"I like that—Tiffany II it shall be."

And Tiffany it was. We felt confident about bringing Taffy and Tiffany in the house, but we knew it would mean some adjustments in our style of living and give us some added responsibilities. It would mean cat food, litter boxes, spaying, trips to the vet, and a host of other things. I explained to Brenda what I knew about raising cats and told her that we would learn much more together. In any event, it meant a new venture for us, but one I was sure that we would enjoy.

Cat Town Races?

The little furballs were still not venturing too far from the back porch. We decided to bring them up in the yard by the garage and let them frolic in the grass. However, the kittens did not like being this far away from their secure home, and they started running towards the porch. This gave us an idea to let them race down through the lawn. Jen and Jo, the neighbor girls, helped us line them up and then call them down to the porch. Taffy or Calie always won the race, with Pewter coming in third, and Tiffany last. Tiff's approach to racing through the grass was a sort of bunny hop. She looked adorable, hopping down through the yard with such a serious expression on her face. She failed to see the humor of these races, but we were laughing hysterically at these cute little creatures running for all they were worth.

We somehow never did get around to naming Coco and Fluffy's kittens. They, along with Calie and Pewter, would later go to new homes. One Sunday afternoon as we were sitting on the back porch, Candy came down from Louise's shed with five kittens trailing along behind her. The three mothers and the seven little ones were there on the porch as Candy introduced us to her new litter.

Brenda looked around and commented, "Do you realize

that we have assembled here four mothers and twelve kittens? Sixteen cats!"

"What an opportunity for a sermon," I offered.

"On what subject?"

"Oh…I don't know…how about 'the perils of being a promiscuous pussycat.'"

"And what are the perils?"

"Uh…they may not go to kitty heaven?"

"Start preachin'!"

"OKAY you foolish felines, you perfidious puddycats, you temptatious tabbies, you…."

"Hold it!"

"Do you think they've had enough?"

"I know I have!"

"Okay, I'll stop…but I don't think they will." And, of course, they didn't.

Some Trial Runs

After deciding to take Taffy and Tiffany in when they were old enough to be separated from their mother, we thought it a good idea to have what we called "trial runs." We began to take them into the parsonage for short periods of time to familiarize them with the house. At first they acted strangely and made their way to the back door, pawing to get out. Gradually, they would forget themselves and play with us and each other and have some food and water.

On one memorable day, we had taken them in and a severe thunderstorm came up. It was one of those windy, noisy, and lightning-filled storms that made chills run up and down your spine. Taffy was not a happy camper at all and ran for cover from place to place—under the couch, the overstuffed chair, or any place she could feel hidden and safe. Tiffany, on the other hand, had been put on my recliner where she laid down for a nap and fell asleep. This little kitten must have been zonked out because she never once flinched during the loud claps of thunder or even changed position. Brenda and I were amazed at how she could sleep through the loud crashing noise that shook the house and rattled the windows.

The two little squirts still insisted on finding their way to the back door in order to rejoin their mother and the other kittens. We knew that this was natural and when we made the move permanently, they would realize that the parsonage was their new home. That time was fast approaching, but just before it came, an amusing incident took place one day on the back porch. Perhaps I should say that it was amusing to Brenda, who still loves to tease me about it. At the time, however, I did not find it amusing—I was serious!

Mama Tyco came strolling in from hunting on a sunny Saturday afternoon carrying her prey, a ground mole. Everything was fine as far as I was concerned until Tyco singled out Taffy as the kitten to receive the kill. "Oh, no!" I cried, and leaped to my feet to catch the little tyke and separate her from the mole. I don't know how long I chased Taffy around the porch pleading with her to stop. Brenda was laughing with tears in her eyes. I finally caught Taffy and tried to extract the mole from her tightly closed little jaws. The little kitten was growling and fighting me all the way, and all the time I was trying to explain to Brenda why I do not want her to eat the mole. By now, however, my wife was in hysterics with tears streaming down her face and not really hearing a word I was saying.

I finally got the mole away from Taffy who was thoroughly upset and who continued to run around the porch growling. Brenda was trying to stop laughing, apologetically, and I was saying something like, "I'm glad you think this is funny. I do not want our kittens, whom we are taking in our house, to eat things like this that are dirty and unhealthy." In fact, I still don't after all these years. Although Taff and Tiff have all their shots, I still do not want them to eat varmints. They get filtered water and the best cat food on the market.

One last note on the mole. Brenda chuckled as we went

into the house. "I wish I had a video camera. That little kitty sure gave you a time of it." Looking back...yes, she did!

Easter is one of my favorite times of the year for several reasons. First, it is the celebration of the Lord Jesus' Resurrection. His great victory over death, Satan, and hell. It assures us of our eternal salvation in Him and the joy of living the abundant life. Easter also signals the birth of spring when nature's spectrum dazzles us with a plethora of colors. Easter is a time of new life. It beckons us to begin again, to regroup and organize our resources, to make another charge at life if we have been defeated and discouraged. And, of course, Easter reminds us of our two little furry friends, Tiff and Taff, who came into the world to become part of our family. And of Tyco, who reminds us that even the worst bully can be "born again" and drastically change for the better. Brenda and I felt favored by God to witness the incredible actions of this little cat who intervened to help and perhaps save the lives of her sister and friend by delivering their kittens.

Chapter 3

The Kitties Are In!

We felt it might be a little too soon to bring them inside, but we couldn't resist. One evening before going to visit some of our parishioners, we officially took Taffy and Tiffany into the house. After discussing the situation and how to go about it, we decided to lock them in the little bedroom upstairs with food, water, and a litterbox. We also made up a bed for them and checked to see that no harmful things were in their reach. Then we proceeded to go on our previously scheduled visit.

Upon arriving home that evening, we hurriedly ran up the stairs, opened the door, and were greeted by two sleepy-eyed kittens who had been napping in the little bed we provided for them. They ran to us meowing and purring as if we had been gone for a few days rather than a few hours. We spent about an hour playing with them before retiring for the night and reluctantly decided to shut them again in the little bedroom until we could come up with something better to keep them confined at night. We did not want them roaming all over the upstairs getting into trouble as kittens tend to do, but we also did not like that impersonal door shutting them in, away from us. Cat experts tell us that one of the things a cat hates the most is a closed door. Being curious and adventuresome creatures, they do not like anything that restricts their inclination to explore and inspect. So we decided to come up with something that would keep them in the little bedroom, but would not block their view of the outside. Brenda suggested a screen about one and a half feet high; so we bought one, and it worked well...for awhile. It worked until Taff and Tiff found that their cute little claws fit very well into the holes in the screen. Soon, they were up and over the barrier and scampering about the house.

The next blockade we tried was cardboard. True, they could not see through it, but they could hear us moving about and know that we were nearby. As they grew, we allowed them to go downstairs but only with supervision. Our furniture, curtains, and other belongings are very nice, and we wanted to keep them that way. Kittens are extremely playful and can be very destructive. Even older cats, if they have not been properly trained, can damage belongings in a hurry. Brenda and I decided that we were going to educate our two little furballs right from the start.

If we caught them attempting to exercise their claws on our furniture or trying to climb the curtains, we stopped them, turned them about to face us, and gave them a firm "NO!" Once in awhile, we would affirm the "no" with a light tap on the nose. At first, of course, they seemed quite oblivious to the discipline, but we persevered. Some people have the idea that a cat cannot be trained like a dog can. This is not true, as has been proven, but it is also a fact that it requires more time and patience due to the cat's independent nature and apparent pride. I say pride rather than stubbornness because cats appear to be very proud and sometimes pompous companions.

On the other hand, "man's best friend," the dog, seems more than willing to do his master's bidding, to be at his beck and call, to obey and to please, and all of this for a mere pat on the head and a "good boy." I have had dogs and loved them all, especially my boxer, which I got when I was 12. I named him Rinny, after Rin Tin Tin, and had him for 11 years. That 85 pound puppy was one of the most lovable, gentle, and faithful dogs I have ever met. He loved children and wanted to be with them wherever they were. (This was contrary to what so many people had told us about boxers being nasty and not liking kids. Well, someone forgot to tell my dog.) I trained Rinny to do many things, and it was easy because he learned so quickly. He often surprised me and my family by what he seemed to know instinctively and by what he learned from us. He was more than just a dog and pet to us, he was part of our family.

Now, back to our cats. Yes, you can teach or train cats to do tricks, obey you, and develop certain behavioral patterns. Once again, the watchword is patience. You must understand the cat's nature, which is basically to do whatever it wants to do. I have often been given that look by my cats that seems to indicate, "You don't really expect me to do that, do you?" Or, "I'll get back to you about that." Being independent and proud—and very intelligent as well—the cat is reluctant to do something or perform a trick just for the sake of doing it. He reasons to a degree, "What am I going to get out of this? What will be my reward for doing this?" The cat knows that the end result of hunting is a mouse; the reward of its patient waiting is a bird; the prize of living with its human is food and water on a regular basis. "So what is the purpose of this feat you want me to perform?" asks the cat. "What is this really all about?"

Having said all that, I am happy to report that we had great success training Taffy and Tiffany to respect our furniture and curtains. I saw the need to construct a scratching post and to acquaint the kittens with using it. I made one of pine wood and wafer board and covered it with carpet. After it was completed, it measured 39" high and 7" by 8" around and had a perch on top. I knew it did not have to be that big at first, but I also knew our little kitties would not stay small for long. They loved it and began using it right away. As they became a little braver, they would climb to the top and sit on the perch. It must have looked quite high to a little kitten, but being up high is an enjoyment for a cat. I guess it gives them a sense of security and no doubt also helps them satisfy that curiosity for which they are so famous.

Like all felines, our cats love to look out windows and watch whatever is going on. In the parsonage living room and dining room, we have sheer curtains along with the regular drapes. We began to teach Taff and Tiff to separate the sheers with one of their front paws when they wanted to look out. Often we would just tie the sheers back, but we did not like to do this when we were not there. We also felt that they should learn to be careful on their own. It was cute to see them attempt to part the sheers and get a claw caught and have to sit there and wait for help. If Brenda and I were near, they would give out a pathetic little meow, and we would come to their rescue. I remember my wife's encouraging words, "Are you stuck? Okay, Mommy's coming." After awhile it seemed as if they got tired of getting stuck, and they would just come to the window and sit there, look at us, and wait for either Brenda or me to open the sheers for them. Once in awhile they would remember that they could use their nose to get through the sheers and that would solve their problem easily.

A Big Barrier

We decided that although they were progressing very well, we would not allow them to be downstairs as yet on their own. After all, they were playful kittens not mature cats. Like little children, they still needed supervision. We were not about to let two little rambunctious kittens loose in our house full of breakables and fragile materials. We had to take some precautions.

I erected a five-foot cardboard barrier at the top of the steps to prevent Taff and Tiff from going downstairs. At first they were content to look it over and pretty much ignore it.

But then the little calico decided to scale it and drop quietly on the carpeted steps and go on down to forbidden territory. I could hear her climbing the cardboard but never imagined that she could get high enough to get over it. But after retrieving her from the dining room table where she was helping herself to some "fuzzies" in a flower arrangement, I decided to watch this determined little squirt in action.

Taffy didn't actually climb over the barrier; she used her sharp little claws to get up to where the cardboard was not tight against the wall and squeezed through between the wall and the cardboard. This wasn't too hard for her to do because our hallway walls are spackled with a rough, pointy texture that can cause a lot of discomfort if you bump into it. For Taffy, it provided an excellent climbing surface and a means for her escape. We could have just closed the door at the bottom of the stairway, but the kittens began to scratch at the door, and we could not allow that.

After recapturing the little feline felon, I would lecture her on the way back up the steps on the virtues of obedience. After all, I am a minister aren't I, and am I not instructed to have my children in submission according to 1 Timothy 3:4? "Kitties are not supposed to be on the top of dining tables nor chewing on fuzzy things which could become lodged in their throats," I explained to my little multi-colored friend, trying to convince her that I had her best interest in mind. Taffy, I think, was totally unaffected by my sermonizing. (I certainly hope my people take my messages to heart more than she did.) I found a more effective way to distract Taffy from the barrier and the fuzzy things was to provide some entertainment upstairs. So I tied some cat toys on strings, got a few cardboard boxes for mazes, and even built them a two-story house with various rooms, carpet, windows, and an inside ramp. They loved the toys and the house, which kept Taffy from scaling the barrier for awhile at least. Brenda also removed the fuzzies from the flower arrangement on the dining room table. This beautiful arrangement was a house-warming gift from our churches and we did not want a little kitty cat taking it apart, no matter how much enjoyment it gave her.

Tiffany's Red-Eye Ordeal

Not long after bringing our little babies in, Tiffany looked like a fellow who had been on a drinking spree. Her eyes became very big and bloodshot, and she looked so sad and sorrowful. Brenda and I felt sorry for this little creature but knew that she would need more help than we could give her.

We made an appointment with the Sunbury Animal Hospital, and the veterinarian diagnosed an upper respiratory infection. We wondered why Taffy did not have it, too, and the doctor informed us that she might be the carrier and therefore would not be susceptible to it. He gave her tetracycline, an antibiotic which cleared up the infection and made our little pussycat as good as new.

While at the animal hospital, the doctor put some drops in Tiff's ears and placed a paper towel over her head. She shook her head quite vigorously, and the medicine flew all over her head. When he removed the towel, he asked us what she looked like. We weren't sure but then he suggested, "How about a gremlin?" Brenda and I looked at each other and agreed. The ear lotion had matted her fur, and with the stiff hair she did resemble a little gremlin, uh...the friendly ones, not the creatures who turn nasty after midnight. We hadn't seen the movie, but we did see the previews. Our poor, pathetic little pussycat did resemble one of those furry critters. I told the veterinarian that I was very happy that Tiffany did not change into a destructive little monster after midnight. He laughed and remarked that kittens can get pretty destructive on their own, without turning into gremlins. We took our sick little "gremlin" home and soon she was back to her active and playful self. We kept an eye on Taffy who never did show any signs of the infection. And neither did Tiffany afterwards.

The Kittens First Trip

In June, Brenda and I decided to take our first week of vacation. The churches I pastor graciously give us four weeks, and at first I was reluctant to take all of them, although our people repeatedly encouraged me to do so. "We wouldn't have given them to you if we didn't want you to have them," many of our parishioners would say. These great people have been so good to us.

Now, however, we were faced with a problem: what to do with Taffy and Tiff. We were going to visit Brenda's parents in Lancaster for a few days, but Mary did not particularly like cats, and Don was allergic to them.

My sweet wife, almost tearfully, said, "We can't go and leave them."

I offered, "Call your mother and ask her if we can bring them along." She did just that and permission was granted.

The two little tykes traveled very well in their pet-taxi and after a couple of concerned meows, settled down and went to sleep. Once in a while, we would allow them free run of the car but that is not the safest thing to do. So most of the time we would confine them to their pet-taxi where we knew they would be safe and not distract me while I was driving.

We took along some of their toys and even loaded up their little house as well. Upon arriving at "Grammy and Grandpa's," these two cuties won Mary and Don over right away. It had been a long time since either of them had a kitten around, and they were entertained by the playful antics of Taff and Tiff. Slowly, Mary admitted liking them, and Don was not affected by their presence in the house whatsoever.

Back when we first got attached to our cats, we were surprised that Brenda did not have any adverse reactions to them as both she and her brother Bill were allergic to cats, too. We thought perhaps this was due to the fact that Taff and Tiff were indoor cats and were no longer carrying whatever it was outdoor cats carry that cause such reactions. One evening we had visited one of our church families, and their cat came in and promptly jumped up on Brenda's lap. He had been outside and the husband let him in. He investigated Brenda and settled down on her lap with his tail swishing back and forth in her face. We made another stop on the way home, and by this time, her left eye was beginning to water. When we arrived home, it was swelled shut. She was most miserable.

A similar thing happened when she handled the cats out back, and especially if she held them up close to her eyes or touched them and then touched her eyes. She used some eye drops that seemed to alleviate a bit of the watering and swelling. With Taff and Tiff she did not have these problems; Brenda could cuddle and kiss them without any adverse effects.

While we were at Mary and Don's, Brenda's brother Bill and his wife Beverly stopped by and immediately were charmed by our two little new additions. Brenda's niece Katherine also came to visit and could not wait to see them each morning we were there. Taff and Tiff were a hit with Brenda's family, and so the two furballs' first trip was a success.

After taking the "kiddies" to also visit my parents, Clair and Louella, who were won over by them, we returned home to continue our adventure with our two little pals.

The Kitties Get Shy

About a month and a half passed, and Taff and Tiff were three months old. Our neighbor's girls, Jen and Jo, came over to see how our new kittens were doing since coming into the parsonage. Brenda and I called them and waited to hear them come thumping down the steps. Nothing! No noise! Nada! Well, we all decided to go upstairs and find the little monsters (as we also called them), thinking that they must be sleeping like two pooped pussercats. After conducting a search, we found them huddled together in "their room," as the little bedroom came to be known, apparently frightened by hearing two strange voices.

It took a while for them to calm their fears and not to try and run for another hiding place, but they weren't totally okay with Jen and Jo being there. We marveled that in just three months they became frightened of other people. It hasn't changed much down through the years either. They will watch our neighbors out the window but disappear if they come too close to the house. If a different vehicle stops out front or comes up the driveway, they run for cover. We wish they were not fearful of others, but we do respect their apprehension and do not drag them out of hiding just to show them off or to satisfy someone else's curiosity. A veterinarian told us, and I have read it in several books, that cats are easily traumatized. The term "scaredy-cat" has a lot of validity. Any loud noise or sudden movement can frighten a cat and cause it to react by retreating or by going on the defensive. Thus Brenda and I have chosen to eliminate any needless trauma we can for our two little buddies.

Taffy and the Q-Tips®

One morning I was at my desk in my study. From there I can see the bathroom doorway and the hallway at the top of the stairs. I had the stairway blocked off again and knew the kittens were upstairs with me. Brenda had started to clean houses for a couple of people and was not home.

I noticed Taffy coming from the bathroom carrying something that I knew was not one of her toys. I got up from my desk, tracked down the suspect, made my arrest, found that she had a Q-tip, and after explaining how dangerous it was for her, disposed of the item in my wastecan. I then returned to my desk to resume my study.

Soon, with my peripheral vision, I observed movement near the bathroom door. I looked up to see Taffy heading down the hallway carrying an object. I went to investigate, and it was another cotton swab. I took it from her and went back to my desk. A few minutes later, I noticed my little feline playing in the hallway with a white thing which she was tossing into the air. Again, I went to investigate, and yes, it was another Q-tip. Once more I separated the cotton swab from the kitten and returned to my study.

As I sat down, I decided to watch what Taff would do next. A minute or so later, she entered the bathroom. I quietly rose from my desk and met the little perpetrator at the door on her way out. She was quick but I was quicker...this time! She had yet another Q-tip. I said to her, holding her right up to my face, "Where are you getting these?" Silence. Other than struggle to get away, she made no effort to answer my question. I walked into the bathroom and noticed one of the doors to the cupboard below the sink was not closed. Upon kneeling down and looking in, I saw that a box of Q-tips was left opened and knew immediately where Taffers was getting her supply. Each time I took a swab from her, she just went back and got another one. What a little smartie! So I closed the cupboard door and thus ended the "Cotton Swab Caper" at that time.

Later on, Taffy decided that she liked "used" Q-tips and went rummaging through our wastebaskets for them. We would find the baskets upset and the contents out on the floor. This happened in the bathroom and bedroom as well. Apparently the scent of humans had some appeal to her because she did not bother with the ones Brenda used to clean the kittens' ears. (This is a regular procedure their "Mommy" performs to remove mites and dirt from the ear canals. I help her by holding them so that we do not cause any injury to their ears. They do not like it, but it is something that must be done.)

As to Taffy's Q-tip escapade, we made sure that all swabs, new or used, were stored securely and disposed of properly. We saw the potential danger of our kitty playing with such items and, like caring for little children, we wanted to protect our furry friend.

It was exciting that day when we took Taff and Tiff into our home and made them a part of our family. We often talk about it and how well they adjusted to their new environment. Like children, it is interesting and moving to watch them grow and change in the various aspects of their lives. Two things have not changed with our two furballs over the years—they love to play and they love to be with us. They crave our companionship and will gladly sacrifice their kitty cat independence to get it.

Our two little friends have taught us many valuable lessons, and we are grateful to them. One important lesson is that we need to spend more time with the Lord and to depend more fully upon Him. Our kitties depend on Brenda and me for the usual things such as food, water, cleaning out their litter box, and so on. But loving and caring for a pet involves much more. Having a meaningful relationship with God does, too. It is more than just reading a devotional book each morning, going to church on Sunday, and saying conscience-easer prayers once a day, and maybe a quick good night one, too. God wants us to talk to Him sincerely and seriously, and maintain an attitude of prayer at all times. Paul said, "Pray unceasingly" (1 Thessalonians 5:16). As we spend more time with God, we learn more about Him, we get closer to Him, and best of all, we become more like Him. We develop a dependence upon Him for wisdom, guidance, strength, and all the wonderful positive virtues that are resident within our God. I like this "dependency." It has no adverse side effects, and you don't have to go cold turkey to get off it. We should consult Him on everything and ask for His advice and leading in all our endeavors. I have found it to be the best and safest way because just as we regularly rescued the kittens from Q-Tips and many other things that could spell disaster for them, God protects and cares for us every moment of the day.

Is God "in" our everyday lives? Perhaps we should give that some serious consideration. He certainly gave us some consideration—He gave His Son.

Chapter 4

Bizz-Balls and Baptisms

I came across Bizz-ball toys years ago when I acquired my original Siamese, in Greenville, South Carolina. These toys are small plastic netted-like balls with a bell inside and come packaged in a bubble-pack of three. The crisscross netting allows the cat to pick up the balls with their teeth and claws. My Siamese used to carry her Bizz-balls around in her mouth and toss them high in the air with her front feet. She had hours of fun with them whether playing by herself or with me. One of her favorite tricks was to push or throw a Bizz-ball down the steps of my apartment and then run after it and bring it back up. She would often push it through the railing and watch it bounce down the steps and either run after it or take her time in retrieving it.

I felt that Taff and Tiff would enjoy playing with these toys, so I bought a pack of them. I had told Brenda all about them and how the cats would love them. Well, one of them did—Tiffany. Our little Tassie was afraid of them at first. I discovered that it was the bell that frightened her, and so I carefully removed it from one of them and this did the trick. Taffy would then play with the ball, and Brenda had a great time watching her and Tiff bat them around. She would roll one through the living room, and to her delight, they would run after it and bring it back.

Taffy finally overcame her fear of the bell and accepted the Bizz-balls with the bells inside. Brenda was thrilled when Taff came in the living room one day with one in her mouth. She and Tiffany did as I had predicted: They carried the Bizz-balls all around the house.

By accident we came up with a new game for the "girls" one day when Brenda found a ball on the stairway landing. Tiffany was napping at the top of the steps, and Brenda called her name and tossed the ball down the steps to her. After a few exchanges, Taffy showed up at the top of the steps, lured from her nap in the bedroom by the action. Brenda called to me to come and see the new game.

Taffy, with her flair for the unusual, added a new twist to the contest. When Brenda threw a ball up the steps to her, instead of allowing it to drop in front of her like Tiffany, she stood up on her back feet and batted the ball with one front paw. This procedure really gave the ball some aerodynamics as it flew down the steps at us. We had to be alert and ready if we threw the ball to Taffy.

I went and located another Bizz-ball, and we had quite a show going on as both of us tossed a ball to the cats. They thoroughly enjoyed this playtime and pretty much stayed at the top of the stairs and let us retrieve the balls. Only once in a while did they venture down the steps, giving into the temptation to chase the colorful and jingling little toys. The steps provided a great place for them to play with us, and they seemed to enjoy being above us like the top man on the totem pole. As one cat expert explained, they are intimidated to some extent by our size, and thus like high places where they can feel secure and somewhat superior. In any event, Taff and Tiff were partial to the steps, and they would often run there and wait for us to come and play, especially if they saw us going to the stairway or heard us going up the steps.

For a long while, the Bizz-ball routine became a "going-to-bed" ritual. We would close the door downstairs and ascend to the landing, and upon turning the corner to continue our ascent, find two kitties laying side by side at the top, ears flat, eyes dilated, waiting for the game to begin. Seldom could we, or did we, refuse to grant their little heart's desire. These two old "softies" usually gave in. However, we learned that the Bizz-balls had to be "put to bed," too, otherwise Taff and/or Tiff would continue the game, or attempt to resume it later on in the wee hours of the night.

One word of caution about Bizz-balls: If your kitties let them lay around as ours do (we have not as yet been able to train them to put their toys away), you will find that they are very fragile, especially if you step on them. Our worst nightmare was during the night when treading down the hallway towards the "necessary room" in bare feet. Ouch! They can hurt even though they are just plastic. Nightlights are helpful, and we have employed several. Still, many Bizz-balls have fallen by the wayside and have had to be replaced.

Baptisms, Commode Style

As a minister, I have certain duties to perform such as visitation, weddings, funerals, confirmation classes, infant and child dedications, ministering Communion, counseling, speaking, and baptisms.

Now, although the two churches I serve are Reformed, I am an ordained Baptist and practice the method of immersion. The people knew this when I became their pastor, and it has not been a problem. In fact, I once baptized nine people in a swimming pool of one of our couples. Others have also indicated a desire to be baptized in this way. To me, it just serves as the best picture or symbol of death, burial, and resurrection. It is a sign or symbol of our salvation by faith in the Lord Jesus Christ. I do not expect our members to be re-baptized if they were not immersed, nor do I deny new people membership if they have been baptized in a different way.

Having said this, I now return to the pussycats and their version of baptism. No, I did not require them to be baptized, nor was it their own idea, but I was at fault in at least one situation.

Taffy's experience came first one day while I was busy in my study. Normally, I put the commode lid down in both bathrooms and the more so since we have the cats. On this particular day, I erred, and Taffy paid the price. She surprised me by running into the study and jumping up in my lap.

I knew immediately something was not right; something was wrong...different...wet...she was WET! I looked down at my little kitty, who apparently had come to me for help and said, "What happened to you? What have you been up to?" And then I saw the soaked strands of toilet tissue wrapped around her body and dripping on my slacks. I knew both of us were not going to like what I was going to do next.

I picked up my toilet-papered tabby and took her to the bathroom where I quickly inspected the commode. Sure enough, not all the tissue had gone down the toilet, so I flushed it once again and put the seat cover down. Then I went to the tub where I began to draw some warm water.

As I stated before, neither of us liked what came next. I carefully put Taffy under the faucet and washed her, removing the tissue as I tried to cleanse her thoroughly. Like most cats, she does not like water, except to drink, and put up quite a struggle. I persevered, however, and came away with just a few minor scratches. Next, I dried her off with a towel and then let her go to resume her play. She ran out into the hallway and shook up a storm, looked back at me as if to say, "Wait until I tell Mommy what you did to me!"

Brenda wasn't home at this time and I knew that she would laugh at this incident. Well, I hoped that she would laugh. Now that it was over, I thought it was pretty funny. Taffy had been "baptized," if only in a somewhat ominous way. The moral of the story was clear: Remember to put the commode lid down.

Tiffany's turn came a little later and happened in our half bath downstairs. Yes, I was involved in this one, too. Brenda was home for this performance which took place one evening. I went into the bathroom, unaware that Tiffany had followed me. As soon as I had lifted the commode lid, Tiff jumped up and fell in, not getting quite as soaked as her sister. I yelled, "Oh, no!" That brought Brenda running to see what the trouble was. She burst into laughter and said, "Well, now they both have been initiated, er, baptized, Pastor. Does this mean that now they can join the church? Or, do they have to go through confirmation, too?"

Standing there, holding Tiffany over the commode, I said, "Very funny! I'll go make out their baptismal certificates right away."

"Sorry," she repented, "But you do have to admit it's funny, don't you?" I had to agree, it was funny. Both of our puddie tats had been immersed, and it seemed ironic that they belonged to a minister and lived in a parsonage.

We were always kidding about raising "Christian cats" and training them in the way that they should go. They would need a sermon every so often along with those father/mother to daughter talks all Christian kids require as they grow.

Our people roared as I shared the cats' unplanned baptism one day in the worship services. Many of them asked if Taff and Tiff would be in the next confirmation class. I kidded back that unfortunately they would have to have their own private class as they weren't too sociable. The kitties' experiences provided us with many amusing discussions and were really good visitation topics.

One of the members of our Zion Church, Betty Jane Renn, who is an avid cat lover, told us of a cat she once had who actually used the commode for its original purpose. Betty Jane was in her bedroom and heard a sound in the bathroom. Upon peeking in, she found her cat "seated" on the toilet going to the bathroom. She wasn't sure that she was seeing straight at first, but she had to believe her eyes, and there was the cat doing its...well, you know.

Betty Jane said that she hadn't trained the cat to do this and wondered just how it came to use the facility. We agreed that cats are great students of observation and this seems due partly to their insatiable curiosity. We know that they are highly intelligent creatures with great memories and no doubt very able imitators. Cat lovers everywhere attest to their remarkable feats and almost human actions. As part of God's creation, they never cease to amaze us.

Betty Jane's husband, Bob, who is not a cat lover, loves to tease Betty Jane and Brenda about their cats. When I told everyone about Taff and Tiff's commode experiences, Bob said to me, "Clair, you missed your chance. When the cats were in the toilets, you should've flushed them!"

Bob and Clair: laughter.

Betty Jane and Brenda: dirty looks.

Then Bob had some other suggestions for Brenda in raising her cats. The conversation went something like this:

"Brenda, now that you are a cat owner, there are some things you need to teach them."

"Like what?"

"Well, you have to teach them to walk the cat path."

"The cat path?"

"Yeah! The double yellow lines in the middle of the road."

Laughter.

Dirty looks.

"That's not funny, Rev!"

"Yes, Clair, that is *not* funny!"

More laughter.

More dirty looks.

"Now Brenda, you also have to teach them to swim."

"I'm afraid to ask how I do that."

"Well, you get a burlap bag, put the cats in it, tie it shut, and throw it in the creek. There's one right across the road from the parsonage."

"That's awful!"

"Okay, if they learn that swimming lesson all right, you have to make sure they are strong swimmers."

"I'll bite."

"The next time you put a brick in the bag."

Laughter.

Dirty looks.

"Ouch! Hey, I bruise easily."

I was the recipient of the smack.

Life has its amusing episodes as cat lovers can attest. Our two pals have provided us with hours of laughter and entertainment, and we often do not know what to expect from them next. This little duo seems to love life and being right where they are in our home. They can amuse themselves quite capably but apparently enjoy it more when we get into the act. Of course, we are happy that they want to involve us, and we are more than willing to accommodate them.

The incidents with the Bizz-balls and the baptisms remind us that we need to loosen up once in a while and have a good laugh. It is true that life is short, and we should not miss anything it has to offer, including some good old-fashioned fun. Laughter is good medicine, and a few big doses of it from time to time will benefit us tremendously.

Happy people are healthier, live longer, are more successful, are nicer to be around, and tend to be the ones who make things happen in this world. They are the people who see obstacles as opportunities and view problems as possibilities. They regard life as a challenge, something to be ruled, not something to be ruled by. They know that God put them here to enjoy life and to get the most out of it they can.

For the most part, Christians are happy people, so wrapped up in the joy of the Lord they don't have time to be gloomy. Paul wisely advises us, "Rejoice in the Lord at all times. I will say it once more. Rejoice!" (Philippians 4:4). The Apostle was not a psychologist, but he knew the therapeutic principles of God. Again, he counsels us, "Offer gratitude in all circumstances" (1 Thessalonians 5:18). As we read through the four Gospels, we see Jesus, traveling about doing good and showing people how to find God. We notice that He is not concerned much with keeping to a schedule, but that He is rather fulfilling the purpose for His life and helping others to do the same. We need to let Him do that for us.

Chapter 5

The Fix Is On!

Around Christmas time, we became aware that our kitties were having problems. Our little girls were growing into womanhood. They were about eight and a half months old and were starting to go into heat. The pathetic "meows" were unnerving, although I had heard them before. This was, however, a new experience for Brenda.

Years before, I came home from college with my aforementioned Siamese cat, Tiffany. I had purchased her at a pet shop in Greenville, and she was now about seven or eight months old. My parents had a Pomeranian named Sam, and these two were a scream. After a few minor squabbles, they became good friends and were quite inseparable.

While living with my parents during the summer, I worked at the mills and Mom "babysat" the cat. One day I came home from work to find a tense situation. I was no sooner in the door when Mom, holding an apparently rattled puppy, gave me the details of my "scarlet-hussy-pussycat's" behavior. Tiffany was in heat and had attacked poor, defenseless little Sammy. The puss was after da' pooch.

Sam slept with Mom and Dad but did not rise with them.

He was a late sleeper, and he was also afraid to get down off the bed. When he was ready to get up, he barked for Mom, and she went upstairs to get him. Well, one morning she heard a commotion in their bedroom and sounds emanating down the stairway that were quite unintelligible.

Mom hurried up the steps and into the bedroom and there on the bed...well, it wasn't a pretty sight. The pussycat had the Pom down for the count. She had all four legs wrapped around him in the middle of the bed, and he could not move. The cat was howling out her mating call, and Sam was just howling for help.

Mom rescued her little baby from the wanton clutches of the promiscuous pussycat before she had the opportunity to corrupt his morals. The kitty was then locked in the basement until I returned home from work. The ensuing discussion went something like this:

"Okay, Preacher Boy, what kind of things are you teaching your kitty cat?"

"Uhhhhh?"

"Your scarlet-hussy of a pussycat tried to seduce my innocent little Sammy. What kind of a preacher are you? Don't you have any Christian influence at all upon that cat?"

"Uhhhh!"

"She trapped him on the bed; if I hadn't intervened, heaven knows what might have happened. What are you doing, raising a lady of the evening?"

"Uhhhh!"

"Well, no harm done. I got there in time before she put any ideas in his little head. But, what are you going to do about her?"

"Uhhhh!"

Then Mom could hold back no longer. She laughed and gave me an hilarious description of my kitty's romantic machinations upon her unsuspecting and vulnerable little puppy dog. We roared over this incident and agreed that it could lend itself to many risqué jokes. Dad could not contain himself when he got home from work and we related the story to him.

It took a couple of days to get an appointment with the veterinarian, and during that time we witnessed some more amusing confrontations between the two of them. My cat continued her sensual attacks upon him, and the poor little doggie did not know what to do. My parents and I agreed that Sam certainly was not a "man of the world," and he had no idea how to help kitty out of her dilemma.

We had to rescue him several times as Tiffany pursued him relentlessly, following him into the living room, the dining room, the other living room, the bathroom, the pantry, the recreation room, and so on. To make matters worse for Sam, Tiffany weighed eleven and a half pounds while he only tipped the scales at about four and a half. She manhandled, or cat-handled, the poor chap.

What a relief it was when I finally got her spayed—for all of us, including Sam. If you have ever heard a Siamese in heat, then you know what I am talking about. What a blood-curdling howl! She often sounded like a baby crying. To say the least, it became very nerve-wracking, and we were happy to help her out of this miserable condition. After recovering from her surgery, she returned to being a playful and pleasant pussycat. I was glad; Mom and Dad were glad; and Sam was verrrrrry glad.

The Present Pussycats Problems

We began to notice some odd behavior in Taffy and Tiff in late December. They were off their feed and unusually affectionate. It seemed that they were two lost souls, not quite knowing what was happening to them or what to do about it. It was both amusing and sad.

Taff was the most affected by their condition. If we petted her she would drop down in graduated levels, meowing louder with each descent. She would finally come to rest with her rear end sticking up in the air. We tried to console her but to no avail.

One day Brenda had some sheets and covers on the floor in front of the washer and dryer. Taffy came into the kitchen and promptly wet on one of the covers. She did this several other times, and I felt it was time to call the animal hospital.

They informed me that this was normal and that our only recourse was to breed them or have them spayed. We had no intentions of breeding them, so we decided to have them spayed.

It was easy to decide which one was to go first: Taffy! She was the one with the biggest problem, so it seemed, and thus she was the logical choice. Ironically, they were in heat opposite weeks so we had no respite from the howling.

Taffy Goes Under

When Taffy went to the animal hospital to go under the surgeon's knife, Brenda and I were like two worried parents with a child that was sick. One of our little "babies" was going to have an operation! Although it was routine, we were concerned.

A couple of days after her surgery, we brought her home. She was somewhat groggy and staggered about like an inebriate trying to keep his balance. We felt sorry for her and tried to help her however we could.

Tiffany did not make the situation easier for us as she hissed at Taffy, apparently smelling the medications and other scents of the animal hospital. Fortunately, for the most part, Taffy either was oblivious to her sister's behavior or just ignored her. Tiff's reaction just did not seem to bother Taffy.

Our little invalid seemed to be most comfortable in our bedroom where she slept on the floor or the cedar chest, which is not too high. She didn't seem to want to leave its confines, so we obliged her by moving a food and water dish into the bedroom as well as a small litter box. She utilized them all and made no effort to go out of the room for a few days. We tried to spend some extra time with her each day to keep her company and reassure her.

I took my study material into the bedroom and worked on the bed, having put Taffy up with me, and she was content. If Brenda was home, she did the same thing. After about a week, she ventured out of the room and even went downstairs. She was getting back to normal, and Tiffany was no longer hissing at her.

Tiffy's Turn

Taffy went back to the animal hospital to have her stitches removed. The veterinarian told us that everything looked good and that she should have no problems. While there, we scheduled an appointment for Tiffany. Again, the concerned parents syndrome emerged. A call from the hospital heightened our anxiety a bit. It seemed that Tiffany was partly in her cycle when we took her in, and the uterus was enlarged or swollen. It was not a serious problem, but it did require a longer incision and a somewhat more involved operation. They would have to keep her an extra day, and when she came home we would have to watch her and give her some extra-special care. No problem! These two little fortunate felines had been receiving special care from day one. We would see to it that she received whatever was needed.

One main concern we had was Taffy's reaction to Tiff when she came home. We remembered Tiffany's reaction all too well. Taffy was a bit more high-strung, a little different, and we were cautious with "Miss Congeniality." You could do almost anything with her and get away with it. Not so Taffy! She would become frightened and feel threatened and try to get away at any cost. So we respected that and tried to give her a wide berth.

Our concern was needless as Taffy welcomed Tiff home with open arms, so to speak! There was no hissing or growling or any kind of negative reaction at all. In fact, Taffy assumed the role of a nurse and pampered Tiff by washing her and licking her incision and by sleeping with her. Tiff seemed to enjoy the attention, although she was even more sedate than Taffy had been.

After a couple of days had passed, Tiff left our bedroom and slowly made her way into my study. Brenda and I watched her carefully to see what would happen. Taffy followed her closely like a mother hen keeping watch over a straying chick. In my study, Tiff tried to jump up into a green stuffed chair but could not quite make it. Brenda and I started to attempt to catch her, but were cut off by a quick reacting Taffy who used her head and shoulders to push her dangling sister the rest of the way into the chair. We were amazed! I said to Taffy, "Some of your mother did rub off on you." (Remember Tyco, the midwife?)

By the time Tiffany's appointment to have her stitches removed rolled around, she was pretty much back to normal. She and Taffy had already resumed their playing and racing around, and we were happy and relieved that their ordeal was over and that they were both fine.

Begone With Ye Fleas!

Later that year, we noticed a common problem with pets—fleas! They were infested with them, and we were shocked at the reproduction rate of these nasty little insects. Those of you who have pets know that you cannot drown them, and they are difficult to squash.

We bought the girls flea collars, but these seemed to have little effect upon them, and their numbers just seemed to increase. Brenda sat in a chair on the weekends during the evening with tweezers and a Styrofoam cup of water, picking fleas off the kitties for endless hours, so it seemed.

The animal hospital advised a flea bath and flea bombs and sprays for the house. (This was years before some of the new preparations on the market that easily control the problem.) The situation was pretty bad, and we knew that we had to do something—for their sake and ours. When we walked through the hallway upstairs from the bedroom to the bathroom, our legs would have several fleas on them. We would pick them off and wash them down the sink or the tub or crush them with a hard object. We finally decided to take some action.

We began by spraying the carpet all over the house and confining the cats to the upstairs and then the first floor until both were done. Next, we gave the kitties a flea bath.

To say we gave this some careful thought is to understate it. We read and re-read the directions until we felt sure of ourselves and brave enough to proceed. The tub was chosen as the logical place, and the process began. We used a bucket to dip the cats and a cup to pour the solution over them, being careful not to get any in their eyes and ears.

Brenda volunteered to hold the little patients while I poured the solution over them. She wore a pair of welding gloves that went up to her elbows, and it was good that they did. The cats' claws were razor sharp, and they tried their best to get away. As we performed the de-fleaing process, I remembered back when a friend gave me those welding gloves out of the clear blue sky. I wondered at that time what I would ever do with welding gloves. As I watched Brenda holding Taffy and then Tiffany, I thanked the Lord for those gloves.

We were both glad when the job was over. I'm sure the kitties were, too. We dried them off and let them have the run of the house; they deserved it after that traumatic experience. We detest anything that we have to do to them that causes them emotional anguish. We know many things we must do are unpleasant but necessary. We just don't have to like to do them.

Bombs Away!

Now it was time to re-spray the carpet and set off flea bombs in the house. To do this we had to go away for a few days and let the spray and the automatic spray bombs do their job.

I called my parents and got their okay to spend the next three or four days with them. Then, after packing our things and putting Taff and Tiff in their pet-taxi, we sprayed the carpet well and began to set off the bombs.

We started in the attic and set off three up there. The cellar was next with two. Each room in the house had one and the hallways each had one bomb set off in them. In all, I guess we set off 18 spray bombs in the parsonage.

After spending a few days with my folks, we returned home and found that our efforts had been successful. There were no evidences of fleas anywhere in the house or on the cats, and there hasn't been since.

Unpleasantness! We all face it from time to time, and it can be quite trying to say the least. Such was the case with having our kitties spayed and de-fleaing them. We have become very attached to these little critters and want the very best for them. I will admit to having prayed for them on different occasions. I find nothing wrong with that, for how many times has our wise and loving Father used animals to help and heal us poor humans?

Isn't it strange that people, created in God's image with intellect, emotions, and will, possessing talents, abilities, gifts, and amazing resources, get themselves into manifold predicaments? Everyone has problems—that goes with life—but many of our difficulties are of our own making. Worry, anxiety, stress—they all take their toll on us. To my knowledge, Taff and Tiff do not suffer from some psychosis, and they do not sit around worrying and fretting about things. Sure, situations may upset them, and they can be easily frightened, but they do not spend their days immersed in a quandary of distress.

God has built into our two kitties, as well as other animals, an instinct of survival and an ability to deal with problems. We are amazed at how they adjust to change and figure out how to deal with difficulties. As noted before, cats are great students of observation, and one of their favorite targets for inspection is these sometimes weird-acting beings called humans. I'm sure they learn much from watching us, and although they may not understand everything we do, they file it away in their memory bank for future reference.

How about us? Are we good students of observation or do we miss so much because our minds are jumbled with cares and worries? Jesus said, "Take now My yoke upon you and learn from Me, because I am gentle and humble in heart" (Matthew 11:29). One of the best ways to overcome "unpleasantness" is to observe the Master in action. See how He applied patience and self-control to every trying situation and did not allow dilemmas to upset or manipulate Him. This great Counselor is still in business and His shingle hangs in the four Gospels. Spending time with Him in the Bible and prayer does make a difference.

Chapter 6

Monkey-in-the-Middle

Taffy's knack for stealing the spotlight has never changed. She continues to amaze us with her uncanny intelligence and understanding. She refuses to do things the normal way cats would do them even when it comes to toys or food. For instance, while Tiffany likes chicken, turkey, or tuna, Taffy wants liver—beef liver that I eat.

Taffy is an innovator when it comes to finding the most unusual items to play with. One day she came across one of Brenda's brand new tennis balls and began to bat it around and push it down the steps. We were in the living room and heard the thump, thump, thump of the ball coming down the stairs but had no idea of what it was until Taffy came in with it in her mouth.

"Where did you find that?" Brenda asked.

"She's like a little pack rat," I said, "but she doesn't leave anything in return."

She dropped the ball in front of us, so I picked it up and rolled it into the front living room. Taffy tore off after it, rolled over on her side holding the ball with her front feet and mouth, and kicked it unmercifully with her back feet. After a few minutes of showing this tennis ball who was boss, she would bring it back to us to repeat the roll-the-ball game again. She also chewed on it, which concerned us a little, but as we watched her, she seemed to spit out any fuzz that got caught on her teeth. We are very protective of our "kids" and try to do right by them and watch what they play with.

The Monkey-in-the-Middle Game

One evening after we returned from visiting, we went upstairs to get ready for bed and take care of the kitties. We always check their litter box and give them fresh water and some fresh food if they finished what was in their dish. If we aren't too tired, we usually play with them for a little while before retiring.

On this particular evening, I finished my "cat chores" and noticed that Brenda was in their room talking to Taffy who was perched on the scratching post. The tennis ball was on the floor beside the litter box, and I picked it up and tossed it to Brenda.

"Here, Mommy, does Tassie want her ball?" It never made it to Brenda. With one swipe of her paw, Taffy snagged the passing ball and brought it to rest on top of the scratching post. We stood there speechless. Then Brenda said, "I think we have a new game—Monkey-in-the-Middle."

After holding the ball for about a minute, Taffy let it roll off the post and watched it but made no effort to go after it. She looked at Brenda and then at me, then at the ball, and at us again as if to say, "Well, are you going to get it or not? Do you want to play or what?"

Brenda picked up the ball and tossed it to me. Taffy watched the ball go past but made no effort this time to stop it. A few more passes and then, just as if she was setting us up, she snagged it again. This went on for about a half hour, and we were having so much fun we lost track of time. Taff never seemed to tire of the game, and almost appeared disappointed when Mommy and Daddy quit so they could go to bed.

At least a couple of times the ball got away from Brenda

and me and went directly at Taffy. We gasped, thinking it would hit her and scare her, but that adept little lady just reared up and caught it between her front paws. She would bite it or nuzzle it a few times and then let it fall to the floor. Of course she gave no indication of making a move to retrieve it herself. That was our job.

The game became a nightly ritual. When we came home from visiting, Taffy would run to their room and scoot up on the scratching post and wait. We usually obliged her and continued to be amazed by her quickness and ability to catch the ball sometimes with just one claw.

We laughed at the serious looks she had on that cute little face, especially when her pupils got so big. We would say, "Intense pussycat!" Any talking we did to her seemed to encourage her as the game went on. I was convinced that she was soooo proud of herself.

The Monkey-in-the-Middle game carried over to our bedroom one night when Taffy let us know she was not finished playing. We had played the game in her room for a while and were ready to retire when the little squirt came in, jumped up on the bed, and plopped the tennis ball down in the middle.

She sat there looking at the ball, then at us, back at the ball, and with a loud meow that sounded like an order, she then swatted the ball over to Brenda.

"You're not taking no for an answer, are you?" Brenda asked.

"She's a determined little twit, isn't she?" I added.

"Okay," Brenda said, "Just for a little while, but then Mommy and Daddy are going to bed."

Yeah, right! Taff had us right where she wanted us. From the first toss of the ball we were having so much fun we forgot the time.

Brenda tossed the ball towards me. It never reached me. Taffy went up in the air and caught the ball with her front feet. It didn't matter how high we threw it, she leaped up into the air and brought it down. She then relinquished it almost immediately and got ready to catch it again. She seemed tireless!

If the ball rolled off the bed for some reason during the game, she made no move to get it. She just waited until one of us picked it up and resumed the game. If she thought we were taking too long, she would let out a resounding "meow" and give us a serious stare. Taffy has an unnerving glare.

Once in a while the game was played on the steps, but Taffers didn't watch herself closely enough when she jumped for the ball. She nearly tumbled over a couple of times, and after that we tried to position her at the top of the stairway where she would be on a flat surface. From there she batted the ball down to us on the landing, or one of us would be at the top with her in case the ball rolled too far away or got stuck under something.

However, of all the places we played the Monkey-in-the-Middle game, I think Taffy's favorite spot was the scratching post. That was where she seemed to run to whenever we picked up the tennis ball. Of course, that is where it originated, and cats are creatures of habit. Like us, they are slow to accept change and our two seem to dislike it immensely at times. If something is out of place or if we rearrange anything in the house, it is given a close scrutiny. We find ourselves asking them, "Is this all right?" What are we saying...?

As I write this chapter, a multi-colored kitty by the name of Taffy has jumped up on my desk and plopped down right in the middle of my papers. She wants some attention, and it matters little to da' Tass that I wish to do some more writing this evening. I call these times "Taffy time" when she decides whatever I am doing is not important and that she should receive my full and undivided attention.

Brenda came in from working in her flower beds, and I called her over to my study door. "I can't do any more writing because "Miss Privileged Pussycat" has made herself comfortable," I complained. A "too bad" was all the sympathy I got, so

I decided to humor my 12 pound visitor and take it as an opportunity to interact with her.

She got down a bit later when Brenda came in the study, apparently thinking that Mommy was going to check her ears, eyes, teeth, or some other body parts as she is often wont to do. Thus Mommy is the "meanie" who plays doctor or nurse to the kitties. They often act like they are being tortured or something worse when she gives them the once over. They fail to see that the inspection is for their own good. Boy! Are they a lot like us!

"Don't Throw the Ball to Tiffany!"

People are alike...people are different. Cats are alike...cats are different. As we watched Taffy and Tiffany grow over the first year, we began to notice that they were different in many ways. For example, we noticed that Tiffy was more gregarious, a social animal if you will. No matter where we were, she wanted to be with us or near us. Taffy, on the other hand, was the more independent type, more the loner. She liked to socialize, mind you, but *she* picked the time and the place.

Tiffany was also the braver of the two whenever we had company. She gave our visitors awhile to get settled in and then would come downstairs to look them over. She stayed far enough away so they could not pick her up, or she jumped up on our lap to observe from a safe spot. If people got up and came too close for her liking, she would retreat to the upstairs or go behind a chair, or run to another room. She usually would return, however, either to satisfy her curiosity or to just be a part of the gathering.

On one occasion, two of our parishioners, Frank and Goldie Ritchie, were visiting with us, and Frank was sitting in my recliner. Out of the blue, Tiffany came running into the living room and was about to jump up on Frank's lap until she saw it wasn't me. She came to an abrupt halt, ran to the kitchen, and slowly crept back into the room, eyeing Frank the whole time.

We laughed and Frank correctly surmised, "She thought *you* were sitting here." We explained that Tiffany would come downstairs, run into the living room, and head right for my chair. She is a lap cat and always likes to be right on top of you. Taffy will get on your lap, but the conditions have to be to her liking.

Another difference between our two little feline friends is their way of playing with toys. If you throw something—anything—to Taffy, she catches it with her front paws. It doesn't matter what it is; Taff just adeptly catches the toy with masterful skill. Not so Tiffany!

We found this out quite painfully one evening when we came home from visiting and accommodated Taffy with the Monkey-in-the-Middle game. After a few tosses to Taffy, we noticed Tiff watching eagerly and seemingly wanting to be part of the action. So I tossed the ball to her as she was sitting on the floor between Brenda and I. Oh how I wish I had not thrown that tennis ball. As I tossed it to her, I said, "Here, Tiffy, catch the ball." She watched as I lobbed it in her direction. She became excited as the ball came closer, watching...watching...watching....BOINK! Right on the head! We were aghast! We did not expect this.

Tiffany, apparently frightened and in some pain, tore out of the room and into our room and under the bed. She huddled there, evidently shocked and stunned, and just out of my reach as I tried to coax her to come to me. I felt terrible and wanted to console my little kitty cat.

By this time Brenda came into the bedroom and was able to reach her from the other side. She really made me feel good!

"Come here, baby. My poor wittle girl! Mean ole nasty Daddy, konked da' baby on da' haid! Are you okay, sweetie?"

"Thanks! That's just what I needed! Are you all right, Tissy?" (She pulls back a little and cuddles closer to Brenda as I reach to pet her.)

"Mean ole nasty Dwaddy."

"Cut that out! I feel bad enough."

"Probably has brain damage…" (Caresses Tiffany.)

"She does not!"

"Gonna have a king-sized goose egg."

"She will not!"

"Daddy doesn't love it." (Still holding Tiffany.)

"I do, too!"

"Daddy wants to bust its haid." (Rubs Tiffy's head and kisses her.)

"I do not!"

"Daddy…"

"Brenda!!!" (She laughs and hands Tiff to me.)

"I'm sorry baby, Daddy didn't mean to hurt you…I thought you'd catch it."

"Well," Brenda said, "I guess we'll have to be careful what we throw to her."

"I know…I wish I'd known she wasn't going to catch it."

"Oh, well, now we know!"

Yes, now we did know, but unfortunately it happened many times again. Tiffany got in the way when we threw things to Taffy; or we forgot and thoughtlessly tossed things to Tiff; or inadvertently she got bopped on the bean just playing around or in random accidental situations. We began to feel that her head had some magnetic attraction for flying or falling objects. Our little accident-prone pussycat was getting her licks.

Kamikaze Kat?

This may be a good place to share how Tiffany came up with one of her nicknames. The tennis ball incident, plus a lot of others, led us to nickname her "Kamikaze Kat." One day in the bathroom upstairs, Brenda had an empty make-up box and was about to put it in the wastebasket when Tiff came in. The cellophane and cardboard made a crinkling noise, and she came running to see if Mommy had a new toy. Brenda said to her, "Tiffers, do you want this? Here." And with that she tossed it to Tiffany, intending for it to land in front of her. It didn't! BOINK! Right on the head, a nice, sharp corner of the box finding its mark. Tiff scooted out of there and into our bedroom, and more comforting and apologizing ensued.

Cats love to chase and run, and our two are no exception. They take turns being the chaser or the chasee and fly around the house at breakneck speed. The first time I witnessed Tiff's Kamikaze antics was when they initiated a chase upstairs from our bedroom. Taff was the chasee this time and headed down the hallway at full speed. She made a quick right turn into the bathroom with Tiff in hot pursuit. Tiff also made a quick right turn...right into the wall! Again, comforting and soothing followed.

In describing the incident to Brenda, I recounted it as follows: "Taffy took off down the hallway like a shot and zoomed into the bathroom. Tiffy followed close behind and zoomed into...the bathroom...almost making it. The wall jumped out in front of her." This happened over and over again as little Kamikaze Kat failed time and time again to negotiate the turns. We wondered if she had suicidal tendencies. I kidded about taking her to a cat therapist.

One morning when the phone rang, Tiff, who is fascinated by the telephone, came running into the bedroom. She jumped up on the bed and went into her "silly" routine as I talked with a parishioner. She meowed and rolled about like a nut for about 15 minutes trying to get my attention. Some cat experts say they think we are talking to them. I don't know about that, but when Brenda calls me on the phone and Tiff is nearby, I let her talk to Tiffany who examines the phone trying to see where Mommy is. On this particular occasion, I looked away from Tiff who was rolling around, and she rolled right off the bed and landed on her back with a thud on the floor. I picked her up and checked to see if she was all right and went on with my conversation.

On other occasions, she fell off our laps, off chairs and the sofa, out of windows, down the steps, off the scratching post, and so on. We came to the conclusion that Tiff was not a good candidate for the Monkey-in-the-Middle game unless we used cotton balls.

What could we possibly learn from a cat playing Monkey-in-the-Middle with a tennis ball? How can a preacher and his wife get so excited about a kitty sitting on a 39" scratching post grabbing a tennis ball thrown in front of her? I know that on my part, I enjoyed it immensely and got a kick out of watching Taffy tenaciously and expertly catch that ball. I am still amazed at a cat's quickness and adroitness in hunting and playing. I am impressed with their ability to pounce upon something or catch an object with their feet. Even Tiffany— who, disguised as a mild-mannered and normal feline, is really that supercharged kitty known as Kamikaze Kat—has become very adept at catching things with her paws, batting them back to you, and so on. God has given cats marvelous abilities, and we should take pleasure in watching and admiring them as some of His most majestic creatures.

Play! It seems like so simple a word that we do not often give much attention to it, but wise counselors advise people to make room for recreation in their lives. It's not wrong to work long and hard, putting ourselves wholeheartedly into what we do. However, everyone needs to unwind and have some fun once in a while. Paul wrote, "Whatever you are doing, from your soul work at it as for the Lord and not for men" (Colossians 3:23). This puts a noble objective not only on our employment, but on whatever we may do. If it is done for God, then it is important, worthy, and should be done well. Solomon tells us that "There is a season for everything and time for every matter under heaven: a time to laugh...a time to dance" (Ecclesiastes 3:1,4).

Play relaxes us and gets our minds off what may be troubling us and lets our souls catch up with our bodies. It helps to keep us from becoming dull and unappealing; it help us to be fresh and enthusiastic. Our two furballs have helped us greatly in this area over the years. God knew they would, and I'm sure that is one reason He brought them into our lives.

Chapter 7

A Heart-Wrenching Decision

There are always problems when you own pets. You can do your best to prevent them and to handle them when they happen. But no matter what you do, you cannot completely eliminate them. Such was the situation we faced one summer concerning the cats' front claws.

I had faced a similar dilemma with my Siamese cat. She had destroyed some things of mine and of others and had scratched a few of my friends. Even as a kitten, she would sleep with me and bat at my eyes when I woke up or tried to sneak a peek at her. Finally, after some real soul-searching, I had her de-clawed, the front paws only. It took a while for her to adjust but she did so quite well.

One of my parishioners, Jane Wetzel, told me of her niece's experience with her cat. It was a kitten at the time and was sleeping with her. She awoke and opened her eyes, and the kitten struck her eye, puncturing her cornea. The initial treatment prescribed did not work and later treatment could not repair the damage. Years later, she still has trouble. I have heard and read of other horror stories concerning what cats have done with those sharp claws to adults, children, and other animals. I have seen the outside cats here near our home with missing eyes, torn up ears, and many other battle scars. It shows you what those claws can do.

The Decision

I have read many cat books and stories by experts and ordinary cat owners alike. The opinions are divided as to the necessity of de-clawing or not. Some of those who are opposed to it describe the procedure as "cruel, barbaric, unfeeling, inconsiderate," and so on. I agree that it is a decision no cat lover wants to make. It is an emotional and traumatic decision, filled with pain and guilt. Someone may say, "What about the cat's pain and trauma?" I am not ignoring that. Any sincere cat owner knows all about it. Surely no outside cats should be de-clawed because it would leave them virtually defenseless. However, when it comes to indoor cats I believe the decision lies with the owner and his or her specific situation. I do not condemn nor criticize any cat owner for either decision. That is their choice, depending on the circumstance.

The first time I seriously thought about having Taffy and Tiffany de-clawed was when Taffy jumped up on our bed to sleep with us. Tiff always jumps up at the foot of the bed, but little Taffers, for some reason, has to come up at the head and over my head at that. On this night, she put one front paw right in my left eye. Thank goodness her claws were not out, but it unnerved me nonetheless. The cats had scratched us on occasion before, either playing or trying to get away when we were examining them, etc. This is to be expected, but as high-strung as Taffy was, and still is, we were concerned.

We also were worried about them hurting each other. They played rough and sometimes it turned a little nasty, especially on Tiff's part because Taff usually got the upper hand...or paw. Taffy is bigger and stronger than Tiffy, and I'm sure it frustrated Tiffers. Taffy developed into a sort of practical jokester and just loved to "ambush" Tiff by jumping on her from a chair or some other elevated object. She would wait for her to come around a corner or under the bed and then pounce upon her, rolling her over and scaring her half to death. Tiff would meow loudly, growl, and hiss, which would just serve to spur Taffy on. I am sure the Taffers lived for these moments. Many times during the night, we would be awakened by the growls and hissing that I am convinced was all Tiffany's. I don't think Taffy ever said a word. (You know what I mean…never made a sound.)

Often during these playtimes, we would also hear a loud thud near our bedroom door. It took us a while to figure out what this sound was. One night before we retired, the cats were playing, and I had closed my study door because I did not want them in there for some reason. I came down the hallway just in time to see Taffy literally throw Tiffy at my study door. This was the thud we were hearing when they were wrestling. Of course, the wrestling match was accompanied by Tiff's long, drawn out growls and hisses. I said to Brenda, who was in the bedroom, "The mystery is solved about the loud thump we've been hearing." I then explained what I saw and what had been going on. Brenda added, "Poor Tiffany!" I then lectured Taffy on the virtues of being a good Christian kitty and told her that one of those virtues was not throwing your sister through a door. Taffy was totally unimpressed.

However, we still feared that with Tiffany feeling quite intimidated by her stronger rival, she might retaliate with outstretched claws and cause some major damage. Taffy was not always the instigator or the aggressor in these wrestling matches, but she usually got the upper hand. She would pin Tiff to the floor and wrap all four legs around her and hold on for dear life. Tiff would squirm to get free, "meow-growling" all the while, and becoming more frustrated as it went on. It was amusing and entertaining to watch them play, but we were concerned that someone was going to get very angry and lash out with sharp claws. Brenda and I made many cat inspections after rough house episodes between the two. We checked for scratches around their eyes and ears and pretty much all over. When possible, we tried to break up any potential nasty situations. Easier said than done!

"Tell-Tail" Carpet Pulls

As the cats ran and played and virtually ripped here and there around the parsonage, we began to notice some pulls in the carpet. The steps and the upstairs hallway were the most obvious. Of course, these were their main avenues of travel, and the carpeting was relatively new. The hallway between the kitchen and the dining room had new carpet as well, and we found some pulls there, too. The dining room carpet was fine because Taff and Tiff did not do much playing there. If they went into the dining room at all, it was usually to hop up on the sewing machine and look out the big window at the front of the house. Brenda covered the sewing machine with a latch hook rug to prevent them from scratching the top, and they loved to lay there and watch the traffic go by. In the summer they would watch our neighbor, Louise, work in her huge flowerbed or Barbara, her niece, set up her flower stand along the road. Or they would observe Brenda working in her flower beds since my wife recently became quite a horticulturist in her own right. As noted before, cats are great students of observation, and they seem to love to watch us humans go through our motions, or notions, of life. I'm sure many of these seem foolish to them. I'm also sure that they are right!

In any event, Brenda and I put all these things together and decided that the best course of action to take was to have our kitties de-clawed. It wasn't a quick or an easy decision. It took a lot of time, and it hurt every step of the way. We consulted with the folks at the animal hospital and set a date for the procedure.

The Operation

We transported our two little patients to the animal hospital, not at all sure that we were doing the right thing. Leaving them there was one of the hardest things we ever had to do. However, we felt it was the best for them and us. We both shed a few tears over the matter. The folks at the animal hospital were supportive and helpful and assured us that Taffy and Tiffany would do fine. They made us feel better, and we needed that immensely. Still, we spent a less than peaceful night with visions of sore paw puddycats in our heads.

In a couple of days our kitties were back home with us, having both front paws wrapped in bandages. It was painful to watch them hobble around and try to get the bandages off. Other than flea collars, Taff and Tiff had never been used to wearing anything, so they tried to shed themselves of the alien articles. Taffy was quite adept at getting her bandages off, and we would carefully put them back on as best we could. We kept a close watch on them, trying to make sure they didn't tear their stitches.

Four days later, we noticed that Taffy was not using her left paw, and Tiffany was not using her right one. So, we packed them up and took them back to be examined. The doctor looked at Tiffany first and found some soreness but nothing unusual. Then it was Taffy's turn and what happened next stabbed our hearts again.

When I pulled Taffy from the pet taxi, I didn't know that she had spread her front paws out to the side to keep from being pulled out. As I finally got her out, she had torn her sutures and was bleeding from both feet. I almost cried right there. The veterinarian took her to another exam room and repaired the sutures and re-bandaged her feet. We were half sick and feeling very guilty. Sad and upset, we took our two little kitties home, hoping that they didn't hate us too much.

At home, Taffy went to work trying to remove her bandages.

It didn't take long to succeed. She discarded one in the dining room and the other in the upstairs bathroom. We called the veterinarian, and he suggested letting the bandages stay off as long as we watched for any bleeding. Both cats would lay and lick their paws, which we knew was good for them to be doing. We did watch to see if they tried to pull out the stitches, and apparently they did not since we found no bleeding or telltale sutures on the floor.

Later, we returned to the animal hospital to have the stitches removed, and things were fine. From that point on, we just had to keep an eye on them and inspect their paws from time to time. We did this and gradually started to play with them to see how they would react without their claws. They passed the tests and, as time went on, didn't seem to miss them.

Soon they were running and playing as hard as before and had no trouble maneuvering corners or jumping and keeping their balance as we had feared. It was nice to let them bat us with their front paws and not be afraid that they would cut or scratch us. In fact, these two lovable little squirts always back off when we gave any indication that we were hurt. Once in a while, they do scratch us with their back claws, and they still stop if we show any sign of pain. We don't have to say a word; they seem to sense if we are hurt. As time went along, we felt that we had made the right decision.

Taffy in the Thick of Things

Taffy's medical record reads like a criminal's rap sheet. When I compared it to Tiffany's, I was amazed at how much longer it was. She is a unique cat, and perhaps things like this go along with being unique. I have no proof of that and would rather call it coincidence. The Taffers somehow finds a way to get in the thick of things. One spring, we found a claw growing back on her right front foot. So Taff was on her way back to the animal hospital.

The veterinarian who removed the claw wrote on her record, "Cat is very good at getting foot bandage off; place up high." How well we knew about Taffy's ability. We had bought little coats for them for winter travel. It took Tiffany quite a while to get hers off, but the Taff? She turned into a little Houdini and freed herself in a flash. Scrap the coats! (They had looked so cute, though, on the girls.)

This time Taffy had no trouble with the sutures and recovered quickly. Soon she was back to playing and being her old self. Again we made routine inspections of both cats to make sure no more claws were growing back. Each time they roughhoused, we were relieved and no longer held our breath, being afraid that one or both of them might get hurt. We still had some mixed emotions about our decision, but nearly two years later something happened which reinforced it to have been a good course of action.

A New Job and a New Problem

That year, Brenda took a job at a chicken processing plant in nearby Hummels Wharf. It was a full-time position, and she had to leave at 6:30 a.m. to make sure that she was on the job at 7:00 sharp. The plant had to be kept cold because of the chickens and never was to be higher than 40°-45°. Some areas had to be even colder, depending on what type of work was being done. Needless to say, Brenda dressed very warm. Her attire would include one of my T-shirts, a complete set of thermal underwear, one or two sweatshirts, several pairs of socks, and thermal footwear. One of the sweatshirts was hooded and went up over her bumper cap, which was required by law. At one point, we invested in battery powered thermal socks that she used when her feet really got cold. At the end of her employment she admitted, "I never did get used to that cold temperature." However, my tough "Trooper" stuck it out for two and a half years.

During this time, Brenda had some difficult problems with

one of her co-workers. This employee made snide remarks to Brenda and tried to cause her trouble in any way she could. Brenda tried to be friends with this young woman, but to no avail. Taffy was so compassionate to my wife throughout this whole ordeal. When Brenda came home from work at night, Taffy tried to console her as best as she could. Brenda would be tired from the long day of work and liked to lay down after supper and take a nap. Taffy seemed to sense that something was bothering her Mommy, and she wanted to help. Bless her little heart, she would purr and snuggle against Brenda and look into her face almost as to say, "I love you, Mommy, don't worry, everything will be all right." Animals seem to sense when things are not all right, and they try in their own way to make them better. No wonder they are good therapy for older people or just people in general. It is said that everything has a purpose, and as a Christian I firmly believe that on God's good green earth there is a purpose for all things, even if we do not yet realize all of them.

One amusing anecdote of Brenda's employment at the chicken plant was the cat's reaction to her clothing, which smelled of those two-legged, feathered creatures. When she would take them off and drop them by the washer, Taff and Tiff sniffed, snuggled, nuzzled, and rolled over the chicken-spattered clothes. Brenda remarked that you would think they were covered with catnip. The cats acted like they were on some drug or were hypnotized by a magic spell. To us the clothes were repulsive, and we could not wait to get them in the washer. Brenda could not always wash her boots, and if she brought them into the kitchen, the kitties would give them the same treatment as the clothes. It was a sight to behold as these two critters of ours enjoyed themselves immensely.

The Taffers

When Taffy and Tiffany had been playing one day, we noticed that Taff was squinting her left eye. Brenda checked it for dirt or fur but did not see anything in her eye. We observed her for another day, and she still favored it so we made an appointment at the animal hospital once again.

Dr. James Temple was the veterinarian this time, and he examined Taffy and found the problem. "Yep!" he said, "Someone had their foot in there. Taffy has a punctured cornea." He also assured us that she would not have any trouble seeing with the eye, but it would need to be attended to. He gave us three types of ointment and showed us how to apply them in Taffy's eye. He made it look so easy, but I knew our kitty and how she does not like anything done to her. The prescription called for the three tubes of ointments to be applied to her eye three times a day for 10 days. Brenda and I just looked at each other and groaned. We were sure her work schedule might also be a problem, but Dr. Temple explained to us that if we applied some in the morning, some as soon as Brenda came home from work, and some before going to bed, it would work fine.

We now had to decide who would hold the kitty and who would apply the ointment. At first I tried to hold Taffy but felt I was hurting her as she squirmed to get free. Brenda assured me that I was not hurting her, but I was not convinced, so she held Taffers and I applied the ointment. The best way I found to do it was to come in to her eye from behind and squeeze a bit of each ointment, pulling the tubes away from her eye. Dr. Temple told us to put about a quarter of an inch of ointment in her eye from each tube. Brenda wrapped Taffy in a towel up to her neck to prevent squeezing her too tightly and to protect herself from the furball's back claws. The system worked well, and we began the 10 day ordeal.

During that time, when Taffy saw us together, she figured out quickly what was goin' down, and she headed for cover. Fortunately, we knew all of her hiding places and were able to carry out our mission. Those 10 days seemed like an eternity to us, but we knew it must be done if her eye was to get better.

Finally, we took Taffy back for her check-up. Dr. Temple examined her and gave her an A-Okay! We were relieved and also glad at this point that Tiffany did not have any front claws when she scratched Taffy's eye. This made us feel a lot better about the de-clawing.

Hard decisions and difficult situations—how they can be exasperating! Such was the case with de-clawing our kitties, Brenda's ordeal at work, and Taffy's punctured cornea. Each one of these tested our character, faith, and patience. When trials like these arise, you hope that your Christian qualities come forth like gangbusters to get you through and even impact others. We know this is why God in His great wisdom allows difficult things to enter our domain.

It tore us up to go through the process of having our cats de-clawed, but we realized that it was a necessary although painful procedure. When Taffy's cornea was punctured, we knew that this situation was going to require patience, self-control, and extreme caution. Each time we had to give her a treatment, we asked the Lord for help. Brenda's situation at work with the woman who refused to be friends was difficult for her, but I had experienced the same thing in the past. No matter how hard you try to be nice to some people, for reasons perhaps not even known to them, they will not accept you. We should not be surprised; there were many who rejected Jesus, the perfect human being who gave Himself for all people. He said to the religious rulers, "And yet you do not desire to come to Me in order that you may have life" (John 5:40). He told Christians to expect ill treatment from the people of the world. "If they mistreated Me, they will also mistreat you" (John 15:20). Our response to them, however, is to be quite a different one. The Master gave this command, "Show love to your enemies and pray for those who mistreat you" (Matthew 5:44).

Chapter 8

Puffs, Strings, and Other Things

A cat can make a toy of almost anything. They are fascinated by nearly everything they encounter and, of course, there is always the call for investigation. Call it curiosity, being nosy, an impertinent interest, or whatever; the cat cannot resist checking things out. Our two are no exception. Bring something new into the house, move a piece of furniture, or rearrange things, and they know it immediately. I don't, and Brenda laughs when I fail to notice something she has changed and says, "Taff and Tiff noticed it right away." I guess that I'm not always the most observant person. Brenda insists that someone could take her and I wouldn't know it for days. I'll give her an argument on that one!

The Powder Puff

Brenda was a cosmetician with a drug company for many years and learned the ins and outs of helping women to look their best. In the Lancaster store especially, she built up a good clientele of ladies who sought her advice on make-up and other beauty treatments. One day she was in the upstairs bathroom "putting on her face" as she calls it and was using blush in powder form. She accidentally dropped the powder puff that comes with the blush and didn't really give it any thought as she doesn't use the puffs anyway. After she was finished, she looked for the puff on the floor but couldn't find it anywhere. Her curiosity was aroused, and she began to look farther than the bathroom. She found Taffy playing with the puff in the hallway. Brenda said, "I don't remember seeing her come in while I was putting on my make-up." I reminded her how cats can come and go without being noticed. Taff, no doubt, meandered in, found the puff on the floor, and claimed it as her new toy. And a toy it did become!

Brenda reached down to retrieve the puff, and the little kitty did not want to give it up. However, Brenda prevailed and then tossed it back to Taffy who leaped up in the air and caught the puff about two feet off the floor. "Wow," Brenda exclaimed, "a Lynn Swann leaping catch!" (For you non-football fans, Lynn Swann was a receiver for the NFL pro-football team Pittsburgh Steelers known for his amazing acrobatic catches.) Taffy reminded Brenda of the great player's ability to go up in the air and make a seemingly impossible reception. She was amazed at Taff's concentration in leaping high into the air and then landing safely without losing the puff. We decided that it was a safe toy for her to play with, and it became her favorite.

Taffy carried the puff around all over the house and would bring it downstairs while we were in the living room watching TV or involved in some other activity. She would plop it down in the middle of the floor and look at Brenda or me as if to say, "Okay, guys, let's play puff!" We usually accommodated her, finding it hard to resist da' Tassy.

Taffy's favorite game with the puff was to have one of us throw it up into the air and give her the chance to demonstrate her leaping ability. She loved to jump high into the air to catch the puff and come down on all fours with it in her mouth. This takes some quick maneuvering to pull it off. Taffy is a master! This feat earned her another nickname: "Acrobat Cat." We wished we could have measured just how high she leaped to catch the puff at times. I believe once or twice she was over three feet off the floor. We do have pictures to prove her leaping ability. Brenda stood in the kitchen and threw the puff up in the air towards Taffy while I sat in my chair with the camera. We have a couple of nice photos of Taff in mid-air catching the elusive puff. This kitty never ceases to amaze us.

At times Taffy wanted us to throw the puff to her while she was sitting on the floor and she would raise up on her hind legs to grab it with her front paws. She initiated a new game one evening when we came home from visiting and had the puff waiting for us on the living room floor. When I threw it to her, she batted it back to me. I threw it again, and she repeated the process.

This went on for some time and Brenda said, "I think we have yet another new game."

"Taffy ought to work for a toy company or something," I answered. "She's good at coming up with new games."

Like many of the other games Taffy devised, the puff game carried over to the bedroom. We were getting ready to turn in and lo and behold, Taff comes running into the room and jumps up on the bed carrying the puff. She dropped it in the middle of the bed and waited for one of us to throw it to her. Of course, a Monkey-in-the-Middle game ensued to Taffy's delight and ours. If only one of us was present, then the game was throw it up in the air, throw it to Taffy, or the bat-it-back-to-you game. When we played Monkey-in-the-Middle with her, there were only a few times that we got it over the kitty's head. Most of the time, we lost!

One night, while Brenda was removing her make-up in the bathroom, I was playing with Taffy in our bedroom. I threw the puff to her, and she batted it so hard that it went over my head and onto the floor. I stooped down to pick it up and when I turned around, Taff had moved to the edge of the bed and was lying flat with her eyes big and wide and her tail twitching. For some reason I sat down on the floor and tossed the puff to her. She promptly batted it back to me. I picked it up and threw it to her again. Again, she batted it back. This went on for a while and I called over to Brenda, "We have another game with the puff, Mommy. You'll have to see this!" Brenda came over and stood in the doorway and watched the intense little kitty play oh so seriously. We had to laugh at those eyes, so open and wide with the pupils so big and black. Smackin' this puff was serious business to da' Taff.

And smack it, she did. The puff went over my head, to the right, to the left, down in front of me, rolled under the bed, and backwards onto the bed. As I watched her play, I coined a new word. I said to Brenda, "Mommy, Tassy can hit the puff with either paw. She's 'paw-bidextrous.'"

"Oh, really?" she responded.

"Yes," I insisted. "She can hit the puff with either paw and sometimes with both. Sign her up with the Phillies!"

We got a big kick out of watching Taffy play with this fuzzy puff, going through the strangest antics to catch or hit it. On the side of the bed, she would often strike the puff several times with her paw, right or left, keeping it in the air for some time. We would say, "That was a double pump," or a "triple pump," depending on how many times she hit it. Our talking to her seemed to encourage her all the more, and her play intensified. Never once did she make an effort to get down to retrieve the puff. Like the Monkey-in-the-Middle game with the tennis ball, she waited for one of us to pick it up and resume the action. If we took too long or were distracted by something else, she would glare at us or give out a reminding meow. I would say, "impatient pussycat!"

Brenda would add, "When Tassy wants attention, Tassy wants attention! She wants to be the sole attraction."

And so we would humor the kitty and go on with the game until she got bored or tired of it or until we got tired and wanted to go to bed. (It was usually the latter!)

Like many of Taffy's games, the puff also carried to the steps. One evening, Brenda started up the stairs and found the puff on the landing. You-know-who was laying at the top of the stairway, and Brenda tossed the puff up to her. Taffy promptly batted it back down to Mommy. Brenda called to show me yet another version of the puff game. We were sure, after this, that when we found the puff on the landing or one of the steps, it was a "plant." Especially if the kitty was perched at the top of the steps with fire in her eyes. She loved this bat-the-puff-back-to-you game on the stairs, and it could go on a long time. If Tiffany showed up to take part in the action, we let her get the puff once in a while if it didn't disturb Taffy. Usually Tiff would take the puff and run or lay down and lick it instead of batting it back to us. Taffy didn't mind playing with her sister, but the puff game, that was another thing. We learned to distract Tiff with something else. Then she was happy, Taff was happy, and we were happy.

If, for some reason, we slacked off on playing the puff game with Taffy, she would subtly remind us by leaving the puff in conspicuous places. We found the little fuzzy thing on our pillows on the bed; on the landing or one of the steps; in the bathroom on the floor; in the bedroom doorway; in my study; once on my desk; on the kitchen floor; on the living room floor; a couple of times on my recliner in the living room; and once right inside the door on the floor of the back room where we always come in after returning home. Taffers was good at leaving subtle hints, and of course, we thought it was adorable.

Cats, like dogs and other animals, learn words and commands. One word Taffy learned very well was "puff." If you just mentioned the word in passing, the kitty was there, front and center. We would often egg her on by saying, "Where's Taffy's puff?" Very quickly the little face would peek around a corner somewhere to see if we really had the puff and meant business. Or, she would come running, ready to engage us in the game. The puff game became a ritual, and Taffy was not satisfied unless we accommodated her. It has continued so up until now. We even take one of her many puffs along with us when we travel to visit our parents.

Strings

Cats, like people, have varying tastes. Taffy likes puffs; Tiffany likes strings. We found this out quite by accident one day as Brenda was walking from our bedroom to the bathroom in her robe and the tie was dragging along on the floor. She felt a tug and looked down to see Tiff after the tie. She continued on down the hallway with the kitty in hot pursuit of the dangling string. In the bathroom, she took the tie off her robe and played with Tiff, who enjoyed it immensely. Soon Brenda was searching for a string Tiffany could call her own. She found one on a worn-out pair of sweat pants and presented it to Tiff, who was delighted. Brenda tied knots in each end to make it easier for Tiff to hold on to while playing or while dragging it around. This string is green and is quite long. Tiffany did inherit a shorter white one, but the green one seems to be her favorite. It goes along on trips like Taffy's puffs.

Now Taffy will play with the string, but if you bring one of her puffs into the action, she will quickly abandon the string. Tiffany, however, favors the string and carries it around like her sister does the puff. We find the string not only on the bed but also in pretty much the same places we do Taffy's puffs. I guess Tiffy is telling us that she wants to start a few playing rituals of her own. Her favorite places of action seem to be the bed, the steps, and the bathroom. If we are playing puff with Taffy, we accommodate Tiffer by getting her string, and she is soon satisfied.

Other Things

As we have said before, just about anything is fair game for a cat to use as a toy. Our two cats love "twisties"—those paper or plastic wires on bread packages. However, these are not safe for cats, and we do not allow them to play with them. Once in a while we catch them with one, but we quickly retrieve it. Another unsafe item our cats love to play with is a rubber band. If we find them with one, we quickly take it from them. Safety pins, bobbie pins, paper clips, and so on must be kept out of their reach. We have all of these around our house in abundance and are careful to keep them in safe places.

Another thing Taff and Tiff love to play with is crumpled up paper. We found this out, again, quite by accident, when one of us crumpled up a piece of paper and tried to throw it into a waste can. We missed—I think it was Brenda—and the two kitties went after it like gangbusters. They batted it back and forth between them and had a ball. When one of them picked it up in their mouth and went off with it, the other one tried to get it away. A real battle ensued, albeit a playful one.

After that, whenever one of us rattle some paper and the cats are in hearing distance, they come on the double thinking that they are in store for a new toy. We usually accommodate them but are careful to watch them so they do not get the paper too far in their mouths. The thought of choking kitties frightens us. After each round of allowing them to play with crumpled paper, we dispose of the paper so that they do not play with it without our supervision. This relieves our minds as well. As one veterinarian/author described in his book, "I have taken nearly every imaginable thing out of a cat's stomach." I have no trouble believing that whatsoever. We have found Easter grass in their litter boxes as well as tinsel. Because of this, we no longer buy real Christmas trees, but for the past several years have used an artificial one. Our Taffy not only went after the tinsel, but also insisted in drinking the water out of the stand. Since we kept our trees up for a very long time, we used Prolong, a chemical designed to extend the life of the tree. It seemed that nothing we did to prevent Taffy from drinking the water worked. We even put bricks over the stand, but that little squirt somehow nuzzled them apart and got to the water. We decided enough was enough and bought an artificial tree.

One of their favorite games with paper was the label on the TV Guide. Brenda would peel it off ever so slowly, and somehow they would hear her. She would then crumple the label and toss it to them with Taffy usually getting the upper hand. Tiffany didn't seem to be as enthusiastic as Taffy about the paper, but if a game was in progress, she would eagerly get involved.

"These are a few of my favorite things," echoes a line from *The Sound of Music*. Over time we tend to accumulate many things, and some become dear to us, especially if they belonged to a parent or loved one. I entitled this chapter, "Puffs, strings, and Other Things," pointing out two of the items that Taffy and Tiffany have converted into toys. "Converted?" why not "turned into" or some other word rather than converted? I guess it's the preacher in me after so many years of using theological terminology.

I know that Brenda and I will remember the "things" in the lives of Taffy and Tiffy for a long time to come. If, in the plan of God, we outlive our two furry companions, I know that a powder puff, a string, a crumpled piece of paper or some other item will continue to hold significance for us. I think we all are nostalgic to some extent, and we treasure our momentos gathered over the decades. They help us remember those we love and miss dearly.

I wonder if any of the early Christians thought to go back to Calvary—after the shock of the Crucifixion—to retrieve the spikes used on Jesus' hands and feet. Perhaps after the Resurrection when their sorrow and despair turned to joy, someone remembered those nails that held the Man of heaven to a cross and went back for them to remind them of what their salvation cost.

After Jesus at age 12 stayed behind in Jerusalem during a

Passover Feast, His frantic parents questioned Him about His behavior. "And He said to them, 'What is this that you were looking for Me? Were you not aware that it is necessary for Me to be involved in the things of My Father?'" (Luke 2:49). What a profound impression this had upon Mary, His mother, "and His mother carefully treasured all these things in her heart" (Luke 2:51). I am very sure that Mary treasured every word her special Son said, every blessed deed He did. With Him in our heart and by our side, we, too, can accumulate some "things" to treasure and treasure them eternally.

Chapter 9

The Big "Cat Spat"

We had been on vacation the week before, and on this particular Tuesday evening Brenda and I had just returned from visiting Thelma Deroba of our Zion Church. Thelma is a dear saint of the Lord who is one of the kindest, caring, most compassionate people I have ever known. Thelma also loves animals, especially cats.

We had just told Thelma how well the kitties were doing and getting along. We shared with her some more of their silly antics and how much we love and appreciate them. Upon arriving home, Brenda checked the answering machine and found a message from her mother. She called Mary while I locked up the back door. All of a sudden a vent screen fell over in the back room and knocked something else down making a loud noise. I didn't know that Taff and Tiff were in there until they came running out at breakneck speed. They ran into each other in the kitchen, slipping and sliding on the tile, with Taffy heading upstairs and Tiffany tearing into the dining room. Then everything got quiet.

Brenda finished her phone call, and we began investigating the situation in the back room. As we decided to begin putting the items we took on vacation in their proper places before any more accidents happened, some terrible cries, growls, and hisses came from the rear living room. We looked at each other and started into the room. I yelled in a loud voice, "What's going on in here?" The kitties came running from behind the sofa with buffed tails, Taffy leading the way and Tiff right behind.

They flew into the front living room, made a sharp left into the dining room, another left down the hallway, never breaking stride, and negotiated a hairpin turn right up the steps and out of sight. You wouldn't think that two domestic short hair kitty cats weighing a total of 22 pounds could make as much noise as a thundering herd of buffalo, but that's exactly what it sounded like.

I went up the stairs after them, continuing my tirade, vehemently scolding them for their unacceptable behavior. When I reached the top, Tiff was in their room on the toy chest, frightened, crying, and wetting on Fido and the cover. Taff had run into the spare bedroom and under the crib. I stood in the hallway yelling at one, then the other, and threatening them within an inch of their nine lives. Big, big mistake!

Taffy Turns Terrible

What happened next, well, I would just as soon forget, but I must confess the result of my mistake. Our little multi-colored kitty went ballistic. Taff began to growl, hiss, wet the floor, and then leaped up against the wall and the window, almost knocking down the blind. I was frightened and didn't have a clue as to what to do. For one of the few times in my life, this preacher was at a loss for words. By now Brenda had joined me in the hallway and was witnessing the scary situation.

We looked at each other quite dumbfounded, and then began to speak "baby talk" to Taffy, hoping to calm her down. It worked somewhat better than my yelling, but not much. Taff backed up against the wall by Brenda's shoe shelf, ears flat, eyes afire, and growling similar to a dog—a mad dog, that is.

We carefully and cautiously approached her, talking softly as if to a baby, not really knowing what to expect from our normally congenial little kitty. The closer we got to her, the louder she growled—a blood-curdling sound—and gave out an occasional hiss and spit. I'm not sure just how long this went on until we finally were able to pet her and get her to come out from the wall. She still growled a little, and we felt that we had made some progress until Tiffany showed up in the doorway.

As soon as Taffy saw her, she began to growl, hiss and spit, and retreated to her spot along the wall. Nothing we could say or do would console her. Tiff slinked away, and our spirits sank in disappointment. We sat there on the floor staring at each other in disbelief, at a loss as to what to do. Our two "kids" had not fought since they were kittens, and when it happened then it seemed like it was over almost before it began. We knew that this was more serious, and it would take some effort and patience on our part to resolve. We didn't know just how much...

Plan No.1: Keep Tiff Outa' Taff's Way

Anytime Taffy saw Tiffers, she went into her "savage kitty" act. She pretty much confined herself to the spare bedroom except to eat and use the litter box. We knew without looking when Tiffany passed by the door because terrible sounds would emanate from the room. One of us would remark, "Yep! Taff's still ticked." We tried a little humor here and there although we were concerned about the situation.

There's an old saying that things usually get worse before they get better, and this certainly applied in Taffy's case. Whenever Tiff came near the room, Taffy growled and seemed to get more upset as time went on. Then we discovered that she was not coming out of the room to eat and drink like she should and didn't even want to use the litter box in their room. We found some stools behind the headboard of the bed and some evidence of wetting on several articles. After discussing some options, we decided to put another litter box and food and water in the room for our cranky kitty. This suited Taffy well, and she stopped going to the potty outside the litter box. She ate and drank on a regular basis and seemed to be glad when we came in the room, minus Tiffany, of course.

Plan No.2: Keep Tiff Outa' Taff's Way

We felt sorry for Tiffy who seemed to be walking on eggshells. She would slowly and cautiously pass by what came to be known as "Taffy's Room," hoping not to incur her sister's wrath. Often she would quietly sneak up to the door and peak in as if to get a glance of her once friendly sibling. She would sit on the steps and peer into the room for long periods of time or lay in the hallway and stare in the direction of her separated sister. At night she slept at the foot of our bed just gazing out the door. I really think Tiffany longed to return to their old relationship before the fight. She wanted things to be the way they were before. So did we! Little did we know it would be a long time before that would happen.

Just as a precaution, we began closing Taffy's door at night because Tiff seemed more tempted to try to sneak in at that time. We were awakened several times during the night by Taffy's loud disapproval of Tiff's presence. Tiffers would come scampering out of the room and down the hall, stop and look back with a confused expression on her face. After observing her for some time, Brenda and I were convinced that she simply did not understand why Taffy was acting that way. She wasn't alone—we didn't understand why either.

Tiff is an easygoing little soul who wants to be with us nearly all the time and follows us around the house like a puppy dog. She is definitely a lap cat and is willing to spread her affection between us. Occasionally she does want some privacy and retires to the upstairs for a while. But for the most part, this kitty wants to be right there with us. It was easy to see that she was afraid, confused, and wanted this nightmare to end.

Taffy, on the other hand, has always been more independent and high-strung. She had been getting a little more social
but still coveted her time alone. You can do almost anything to
Tiffy, but not so with Taffy! She feels threatened when you
pick her up and can become quite adamant about getting free.
We have not pushed the issue; we love her up a little and let
her go. We do not want to upset the apple cart, so we have
treated this "fragile feline" with kid gloves.

Plan No. 3: Try to Pacify the Perturbed Pussycat

Each morning we would go into the spare bedroom to say
hello to our distraught kitty, talk to her and pet her, check her
food, water, and litter box, and let her know that we were not
upset with her. She was affectionate, but still a little distant
and ever keeping an eye out for Tiffany.

After Brenda left for work on the days she had cleaning to
do, I would periodically check on our troubled kitty from my
study. I tried also to know where Tiffy was most of the time so
that I could intervene in case of a confrontation. I knew one
thing—I was not going to raise my voice. I had learned my
lesson the hard way.

If Brenda worked until noon, we would check on the little
squirt together and spend some time reassuring her that she
was safe and secure. I think that is important to cats because
they are easily traumatized and are very intelligent creatures
with excellent memories. Taffy happens to be a cat that requires some special care and consideration. This is not unlike
some people who need to be handled with TLC. Notice the
Apostle Paul's words in 1 Thessalonians 5:14. He did not lump
everyone into one category and advise the same treatment for
all. No, he prescribed special care for some who needed it.
Animals are the same way.

If Brenda worked later, I would check on Taffy myself and
spend a little time with her before going out on my afternoon
visitation. As is my usual practice, I would leave a note for

Brenda telling her where I would be and any special information about Taff, etc. We would repeat the above after supper and at night after coming home from visitation. We didn't worry too much about another fight at this point because Taffy was not venturing out of the spare bedroom, and Tiff was giving her a wide berth. It was quite an experience for us with these two pussycats who had gotten along well up to this point. We were not quite sure what to do about this situation, but we wanted to do the right thing.

Counseling for Cats: Is the Doctor In?

After a few weeks of observing our troubled kitty and seeing no change in her attitude toward her sister, we decided to ask for some help. We called our friends at the Sunbury Animal Hospital, and they told us that our situation was not unusual. Cats are excitable creatures and sometimes are easily upset. They said to give it some time, amuse and pamper the pussycat, and do our best to keep her from becoming more traumatized. What they didn't know, and we didn't know, was how long it was going to take Taffy to recover.

We were a bit reluctant to tell our friend Thelma about our problem after bragging so much about them the very day the problems all began. But we knew that she would understand and be eager to help. Thelma agreed with the animal hospital that Taffy would have to work it out of her system and that we should allow her some time and not try to push her. She did give us a brochure on a veterinarian in the Harrisburg area who offered counseling in person and over the phone. We considered this possibility, but then decided not to go that route.

I also talked with another friend, Barbara Bolig, who has seven cats of her own and who has faced about every problem cat-lovers come up against. Barb tells us that she has upstairs cats and downstairs cats and never the twain do meet. A couple of her cats just do not like each other, and Barb and her husband Jim have had to separate them more than a few times. Barb uses a broom handle, and Jim uses his cane. We both had read of the waterbottle spray method, which is effective and harmless to the cats. Just don't spray the water on their heads, avoiding their eyes and ears.

Barb advised us to be patient, give both cats a lot of love and assurance, and respect their personality differences. When you love your pets and consider them part of your family, you will make the necessary concessions to keep them happy and as trauma-free as possible.

We also borrowed Thelma's cat therapist book and reread the sections pertaining to our particular problem. I shared this with both our congregations that I was counseling the kitty cats and they roared. I told them that a pastor never knows just what he may find himself involved in. He has to be prepared for anything.

The author of Thelma's book suggested allowing the cats to work things out themselves and to talk softly to them at all times. If they started to have a problem, say things to them like, "Are you guys okay? Is everyone okay?" It does help. Our cats know the word "Okay" because we call up the stairs to them after company leaves or they have been frightened by something, "Taffy, Tiffy—it's okay." Often they come down right away because they know that means it's all right, and it's safe. Of course, no one would hurt them and the "things" that frighten them include sirens, loud trucks, low flying jet planes, people talking outside, and so on. Thus we began using a "speak softly" technique even when we were not necessarily talking to them. It helped, and we still apply this method today. It's understandable; cats do not care for noise and clamor and that explains why they often go and hide somewhere or retire to a secluded spot. Good idea—even for us humans. Does not God tell us to be quiet, to find quiet places, and to relax silently? Of course, and we need to do it more often. Both cats and people need quietness.

We Want Our Sweet Wittle Taffy Back

It wasn't pleasant almost tip-toeing around Taffy in her disturbed state of mind. We began feeling afraid of doing something that would set her off. Gradually, however, although continuing our speak softly policy, we went about our business on a normal basis. We still spent time with her at regular intervals throughout the day and with Tiff as well.

Brenda said one evening, "I want my sweet wittle Taffy back!" I knew what she meant. She was reminiscing about our kitty's cute antics over the years. We couldn't help but remember those happier times when Taffers was a scream and either had us in stitches or was melting our hearts.

When she was still a kitten, she would crawl up on Brenda's right shoulder as Mommy was lying on the couch. She would take her paw and carefully push Brenda's hair back away from her ear and nuzzle closer, purring profusely and often licking her ear. This would go on for a long time, and I applauded my wife for her patience and sacrifice on her kitty's behalf. She would wince once in a while when that rough little tongue went over her ear, but she put up with it. Just exactly what Taffers got out of this ritual we do not know, but she kept it up for quite a while.

One year I had an esophageal attack and thought I was having a heart attack. I was admitted to Sunbury Hospital for tests and observation for a few days, and one of our members had some cute balloons sent to me. I took them home, and we had fun watching Taff and Tiff follow them around as the air currents in the house shifted. As with all balloons, in a couple of weeks the helium leaked out, and they floated lower and lower, coming close to the floor. The cats weren't too sure about this; but their curiosity got the best of them, and they had to investigate. On one occasion, Taffy got too close and a string caught her tail. At this time the balloons were upstairs, and I was in the kitchen doing something. I heard a ruckus like thunder and turned to see Taffy come running from the stairway into the kitchen, turn and look back at the partially closed door. We keep the door that way when the weather turns cooler to help prevent the heat from going upstairs. I walked over to the door to see what was scaring the kitty. There wedged in the door were balloons. Taffy had dragged them down the steps as if being pursued by a host of attackers. I laughed as I reached down to console my frightened feline. "Did those nasty balloons almost get my Tassy?" This did little to assuage her fear, and she was not content until I removed those dastardly demons of gas. When Brenda came home from work, I had to tell her about Taffy's escape from the "bad balloons." She picked up her little darling and said, "Did those nasty things hurt my wittle baby?" By this time, I'm sure that Taff had forgotten about the incident, but she ate up Mommy's attention.

This was the "cute" Taffy we wanted to see again. We knew that it would possibly take some time, some patience, and a lot of love. We were willing to do it because we felt our kitty was worth it.

Thanksgiving: Home Alone I

This was one of the toughest things we ever had to do in regard to our kitty cats. Thanksgiving time was drawing near, and we had made plans to travel to Brenda's parents for the holiday. However, with Taffy confining herself to the spare bedroom and going berserk every time she saw Tiffany, you might say we had some reservations about taking her along. But what were we going to do? We couldn't leave her, could we? That would be a very difficult thing for both of us to do. Yet, we could not imagine trying to put Taffy in a pet taxi, let alone dealing with everything that could happen at Mary and Don's. So, after much discussion and many tears, we decided to leave our kitty at home.

We have five litter boxes—three regular ones and two

covered. We take the smaller covered one when we travel to our parents. So we filled four of them with kitty litter and spaced them in the kids' room along with several dishes of food. We purchased a three liter, gravity-fed water dish and positioned it so Taffy wouldn't knock it over if she happened to get rambunctious. Lots of bedding was provided for the kitty who was to go solo for the first time in her six and half year life. We had left our two little pals alone for a whole day several times before, but this was a new experience. We knew it would be tough.

As we pulled out of the driveway, I think Brenda was having more trouble than I was. It was a quiet, quiet drive to Lancaster that day. From time to time we reassured each other that Tassy would be okay. We even prayed that our loving heavenly Father would watch over our little puddie tat. Okay, okay, so we go to extremes sometimes. It made us feel better.

We explained the situation to Grammy and Grandpa Barnett, and they agreed that we had made the right decision. It sure seemed strange not to see the little multi-colored kitty in the spare bedroom or see her sneak out at night, prowling around the apartment. Tiffany got all the attention for once and loved it. She came out and sat with us most of the day when we were in the living room. If Brenda and I went back to the spare bedroom to take a mid-afternoon nap, Tiff would come and join us. Wherever we were, she was right smack-dab in the middle.

When it was time to go home, we didn't know quite what to expect or what we might find. Upon arriving at the parsonage, I decided to go upstairs alone and check on Taffy. We had closed the door to the steps, thinking it best to confine her to the second floor. I slowly climbed the stairway and peeked in the room. Taff was lying on the toy chest with Fido, the stuffed dog. She looked up and then put her head back down, not apparently excited about seeing me. I was a little hurt that my kitty did not seem glad to see me. Brenda received the one-glance treatment, too. When Tiffany came up, Taffy stiffened and looked at her with dark, angry eyes.

An incident about two weeks before Thanksgiving had reinforced our decision to leave our multi-colored kitty at home. We went to a concert at one of the local Sunbury churches and then to a restaurant afterward. It was Saturday night, and we are not usually up late because of church the next day. But we decided to treat ourselves on this rare occasion and arrived home close to midnight. We went upstairs and began conversing with Taffy who was still pretty much confining herself to the spare bedroom. She was sleeping behind the little fold-up couch and when Brenda picked her up, she noticed some stools on the strip of carpet Taff layed on. My wife held the kitty up to her face and scolded her saying, "And what is this? Are we too lazy to walk to the litter box?" Taffy flipped! She hissed, she spit, she growled, she struggled, and she jumped out of Brenda's arms. I quickly asked my surprised spouse, "Are you okay? Did she scratch you?" Brenda acknowledged that she was all right, and we began trying to console our angry little feline.

She would have none of it. She ran from one hiding place to another growling like a dog, hissing at us whenever we came close. Her eyes were big and black, her ears were flatter than a Scottish Folds', and she was not in a good mood. If she saw us, she growled; if we talked to her, she growled; if we talked to each other, she growled. Finally, after many attempts of coaxing and comforting, Taffy ran into the cats' room, and we shut her in. Poor little Tiffy was content to observe all of this from under our bed. After some careful thought, we nearly decided to join her.

The confinement to the cats' room lasted three days. During that time we made sure Taffy had food and fresh water and a clean litter box. We were always greeted by growls and hisses, usually from on top of the toy chest or under it. She did eat and drink and use the litter box, most of the time. We did find some stools on and under the toy chest, but neither one of us complained to Taffy about it.

On one occasion I decided to peek in on our cranky cat and I just opened the door without saying a word. I had it open just a few inches, I was greeted by a loud hiss, so I said, "Okay," and closed the door. Brenda came up behind me and exclaimed, "I guess she's not ready to make up with us yet." I agreed and we left Taffy alone for a day or so.

Finally, I decided enough was enough, and I told my wife of 11 years to get ready to call our good friend, Jerry Blank, a local mortician, because "I was goin' in!" Me and Miss Kitty was gonna' have it out, face to face, ole-fashioned style! I opened the door and the hissing and growling began. Taffy was lying on the toy chest, ears flat, eyes afire. She was looking straight at me as I walked slowly toward her. The closer I got, the more intense the growling became. Brenda, standing behind me, said, "Be careful." I kept going, slowly, ever so slowly, reaching out my hand toward the Taffers. I decided I was going for broke.

I reached toward her head, speaking softly and reassuring her all the while. I kept talking to her as I began to pet her. At first she growled more loudly. However, I continued consoling her and petting her. Finally, she calmed down and quit growling and became quite subdued. Brenda came in the room and began to talk baby talk to her and pet her. Taffy ate it up. I cautioned, "Just don't try to pick her up." With the situation already quite fragile, I didn't want it made any worse.

Our coddling and cooing seemed to work as Taffy began purring and nuzzling. How glad we were to hear that sound again. It was like beautiful music compared to the hissing, spitting, and growling. We were not presumptuous to think that things were back to normal. As soon as Taffy spotted Tiffany, she went into her defensive mode. We continued talking softly to her, telling her that it was okay. At least she didn't begin her nasty cat act again, but we knew that it would take some careful maneuvering on our part to keep things on an even keel. We tried to make sure that the two cats could keep out of each other's way. Eventually, Taffy sort of claimed the spare bedroom and the cold cat war continued.

Christmastime: Home Alone II

It has been a Christmas tradition for years: My parents usually have the family Christmas party the second Saturday in December. Ever since we had been with the churches, I scheduled the Lord's Supper to be held on the first Sunday of December and had a guest speaker to fill in on the second Sunday so that we could go to the party. We had made plans far in advance and really wanted to go to the party and be with the family. Mom and Dad used their church's basement since their house was too small to accommodate Mom's growing clan. It was always a great time of fun, food, and fellowship. When my Mother was ill a few years ago and could not have the party, everyone missed the family get-together. She resumed it after a couple of years, much to the delight of all.

So, needless to say, Brenda and I wanted to attend the party, but once again, a gut-wrenching decision was in order. The question was, to take Taffy or to not to take Taffy. Once more we talked it over and decided not to take our little feline in her frame of mind. Yes, once again we faced a terrible time of mixed emotions. But, in the end, reason won over emotion, and we left our Tassy at home on another five-day stint.

We had a great time visiting with my parents and family at the Christmas party, but we still had sad thoughts of our Taffy. We were not used to leaving our kitties behind, and the first time did not make this one easier. Our reception by the little squirt was about the same as that at Thanksgiving when we arrived home late Sunday afternoon. Taffy may have been a little happier to see us this time, but I won't exaggerate. She was definitely not glad to see Tiffany and continued the cold war.

The Spat Goes On

We thought that any day now Taffy would forget about her tiff with Tiff and things would get back to normal. Wrong! Our kitty was not easily assuaged. She continued to use the spare bedroom as her headquarters and rarely ventured outside its confines. It was sad to see Tiffy sit outside the door and look in. We could just tell that she longed to have things back the way they once were. However, if she did venture in and Taffy saw her, she was greeted by a hiss or growl. Tiffy did not stay around for more mistreatment. She exited quickly, usually turned around and looked back, hurt and confused. Brenda and I would try to console her as best we could and give her some extra attention. We figured it would be a waiting game, but we continued to coax Taffy to get her to come out of the room. "Lord, give us patience, and we want it now!" was our desperate cry.

Before we knew it, a new year was upon us and not much changed in the "Taffy" situation. She did seem more amicable toward Brenda and me, but not with Tiffers. We were careful not to raise our voices and make the situation worse. It was like walking on eggshells, and we grew tired of this after awhile. We decided to be normal, positive, and let things take their course.

Time went on, and one evening as we began retiring for bed, Taffy came into our bedroom and jumped up on the bed. I was so surprised I yelled, "Taffy!" Brenda was in the bathroom and wondered what was going on. Almost immediately Taffy leaped off the bed and ran back to the spare bedroom, either startled by my outcry or that she forgot herself. It was the first time that we had seen her in our bedroom since the spat. I felt badly about crying out, but Brenda said she thought that the problem was more that Taffy forgot herself. Good wife, making her hubby feel better.

It would be about a year before our kitty ventured downstairs. She had by now become civil to Tiffany and wandered freely about the upstairs. She was on her way to becoming our old Tassy, and we continued to coax her downstairs. She began by coming down to the landing and meowing to get our attention. Of course, you probably guessed, we spent a lot of time on the steps coddling and coaxing our kitty. We decided to be patient and play it her way, all the time encouraging her to join us in the living room. She would come down to the hallway but no farther than that.

One evening, I was washing dishes (lady readers, did you catch that?), and I saw movement out the corner of my eye and I turned to see Taffy slink into the back room. Once again my emotions overruled my thinking and in my delight I cried out, "Tassy!" The kitty stopped abruptly and ran back up the steps. My heart sank! I looked in at Brenda who was sitting in her chair and sadly exclaimed, "Booders! I blew it! The first time Taffy comes down when we were here and I have to goof up!" My dear wife was understanding, and she consoled me by reassuring me that Taffy would come down again. "She got her feet wet and now the next time will be easier," Brenda reasoned. She was right. In the next few months, Taffy came down to the kitchen several times but still would not go into the living room. In fact it would be a year and a half before she got back to her old self and started to roam through the entire house.

It happened one morning as I was getting ready to eat lunch. I sat down in my recliner to turn on the TV and, lo and behold, Taffy came into the living room. She jumped up on the couch and came across to Brenda's chair, hopped over on my lap and then onto the stepstool at the window. She sat there a few minutes, looking out a window she had not graced with her presence for a year and a half and then came back over onto my lap, curled up, and snoozed a bit. I was elated to say the least, and it was all I could do not to jump up and call Brenda at work with the good news. I restrained myself, however, and waited until she came home. My wife was elated, too, and somewhat relieved. We both hoped it would last.

A Permanent Breakthrough

It did last, and as I write this chapter, the two cats have gotten along well these past three years. Sure, once in a while we hear a hiss, a growl, see a paw adeptly placed in someone's face, or a chase down the hallway, but we respond with our patented, "Is everyone okay? Tissy, Tassy, okay?" This more subdued approach has worked and usually settles things before they become serious. Proverbs 15:1 says, "A soft answer turns away wrath." We determined to refrain from any loud outbursts when the two kitties had a disagreement. This, of course, is what we should have been doing all along. Since cats are easily traumatized, our boisterous reprimands only made matters worse. We should have known better.

However—and this is not meant to be an excuse—the ministry can be stressful and cause a great deal of tension. That tension can be felt by people and pets alike. Neither of them care to be affected by it. I don't, and I am sure no sane, normal person does. So Brenda and I learned something—or were reminded of something—not to allow pressure and anxiety rule our lives. Peter advises, "Shift all your anxieties upon Him, because He is concerned about you," 1 Peter 5:7. "You will keep him in perfect peace whose mind is kept firm on You" is good counsel from Isaiah 26:3.

Yes, it is easier to preach it than to practice. Through two kitty cats, God got through to us—especially me—to slow down a bit and to take life in stride and to trust Him for everything. Are we doing it perfectly? Of course not! But even when our families and our parishioners are sick, having problems, or are called to their eternal home, we are handling it better. I have found that my prayer life has improved, my personal life is smoother, my preaching, which has always been great (just kidding), has more positive pizzazz, and my outlook on life in general is more optimistic and filled with a sense of expectancy. My faith in God is stronger, and I look to Him for great things. I am happy, the cats are happy, and I think my loving Lord is happy with us.

Chapter 10

Tiffany, Our Little Sweetie

It is true that children take on characteristics of their parents. This includes physical features, of course, but also personality traits as well as other peculiarities. I believe that this applies to animals, too. We have observed that our two cats display some distinct characteristics of their family members. Tiffany is like her mother, Tyco. Taffy, on the other hand, takes after her Aunt Smokey.

Like Mother, Like Daughter

I explained in chapter two that Tyco, our cats' mother, was the runt of the litter. She made up for it by being aggressive and going on the offensive. She terrorized her sisters at mealtime and controlled them with her ferocious behavior. Tiffany is by no means a runt at 11 pounds, but she is smaller than Taffy who gets the best of her sister in a wrestling match. As I mentioned previously, Taffy is very strong, as was her Aunt Smokey. Holding Tiffy when she is trying to get free is easy compared to hanging onto the Taffers.

Like her mother, Tiffany became a "bully" at the feeding dishes. In their room, we provided two food dishes and a large water dish. One evening, after refilling the dishes with food, we noticed that Taffy was acting sheepishly and not eating. I went over to her, petted her, and said, "Tassy, are you okay? Are you feeling all right? Go ahead and eat." I'm sure she understood every word. Thinking that everything was copacetic, I left the room. Shortly, Brenda called to me, "Clair, come here."

I came back slowly and peered into the room just in time to see Tiffany swat at Taffy and growl at her as she tried to eat. My next move was to scold Tiff, swat her backside, and tap her on the forehead with my finger. The cats were not very old at this time, and I felt we had better stop the behavior right away. It took a while to break the little kitty of this practice, but finally she quit bullying her sister. In fact, I felt somewhat like a bully myself as Tiffy became very timid and would not go near the feeding area. Eventually, she got back to normal with some coaxing and reassuring. She did not, however, resume the nasty behavior, which made us all very happy.

"Tiffany...Talk!"

The little gray and white kitty was sort of quiet even though she wanted to be where you were. She would follow us around from place to place and just sit and stare at us. Sure, often she would try to get on our laps or get closer to us but at the same time she would hardly offer a single meow. Taffy, on the other hand, was quite talkative at this time. Did our little feline have a problem? Did I, by my discipline, inhibit her from being a normal, well-rounded pussycat? I began to feel guilty about this situation and discussed it with Brenda.

My wise wife suggested that we talk to her, specifically direct our conversation to Tiffy. Made sense. People talk to their pets, their plants, their possessions, and themselves. Tiffany qualified as a pet, so we decided to make a concentrated effort to get her to talk. So whenever she came around and we remembered, we said to her, "Tiffany...talk!" We kept this up for some time and the kitty caught on. Soon, our heretofore quiet little furball was talking up a storm. We were quite proud of ourselves and enjoyed having Tiff carry on a conversation with us. She would join us in the living room, or wherever, and begin to meow profusely. For a long time, this was amusing to us as this little gray and white pussycat sat staring at us so seriously trying to communicate with us. However, if we were talking, reading, watching TV, or just napping, it did become a little annoying.

When I complained, Brenda reminded me, "You wanted her to talk!"

I responded, "Yes, yes...but not when I'm trying to concentrate on something."

"Oh, sure, she's supposed to know when you are not busy, is that it?" My wife came back at me.

"Well," I conceded. "I guess not. I shouldn't expect her to know the difference. She's only a cat!"

"That's right, and a pretty smart one at that," added my better half. I had to agree!

To this day, at nine years of age, our little kitty still loves to talk and has become quite adept at talking back, especially to Mommy. This happens mostly at bedtime when Brenda says to her, "Okay, Tiff, let's go to bed."

Tiffers may be lying on a chair, her favorite stool, the floor, or some other frequented spot, and her usual response sounds like a "nnnick" or a "nnnyip." Nothing resembling a meow! As long as Brenda talks to her in a normal tone, Tiff continues to answer with these short, distorted sounds and makes no effort to move. Then mean ole nasty Mommy gets tough! In a louder and firmer voice, she demands, "Tiffany...up!" Now the kitty moves, nnyicking and nnyiping all the way to the bottom of the stairway where she stops and sits down.

Brenda steps out into the kitchen and asks her, "Are you ready to go up to bed now?" More sass from the furball. Mommy moves closer, trying not to laugh, and orders the defiant feline, "Up!" After some more back talk, Tiff goes up the steps nnyick, nnyick, nnyicking the whole time. Sometimes she stops on the landing and talks up a storm until one of us starts up the stairway. Then she runs to the top and looks down, continuing her almost half-hearted imitation of a gag sound. Her next move is normally to zip into our bedroom and jump up on the bed, roll over and go into her, "Aren't I an adorable and pretty little kitty?" routine. We have to admit she is both of those things.

Tiffany and the Telephone

Another phase of "Tiffany talk" is our kitty's escapades with the telephone. For some reason, she runs to it the moment it rings. No matter where she may be in the house, when our three telephones ring, Tiff usually runs to the one closest to where Brenda and I happen to be. Once in a while, if she is downstairs she will go to that one even if we are in the bedroom or the study. Most of the time, however, she comes to the phone we answer and begins her own conversation. This can get somewhat annoying when you are trying to talk and listen and a kitty cat is meowing quite loudly close by. If she makes too much of a nuisance of herself, we have to shoo her away without being nasty. We think this is cute, but when we have an important phone call, we cannot be interrupted by a persistent pussycat.

Often we find her by the answering machine in the living room when we come home from visiting or from someplace else. Tiff is intrigued by the voice, I guess, and often sits on the arm of the sofa meowing at the machine. One of our parishioners suggested we train her to answer the phone. Quite a trick if we could pull it off. We're not sure why this little cat is fascinated by telephones and their accessories. Someone offered a theory that when we are talking on the phone they think we are talking to them. That is plausible, I suppose, but I often hold the phone for Tiff to listen to Brenda and it is evident that she recognizes Mommy's voice. She can't quite figure out how her Mommy got in the telephone. She nuzzles the receiver and listens inquisitively as Brenda talks to her.

Once, when I was in the bathroom upstairs, the phone rang and the call was for Brenda's mother, Mary, who moved in with us on her 80th birthday. I called down to Brenda to give Mary the phone and listened to hear when Mary answered. The call was about a raffle Mary had won at a local restaurant, and she knew nothing about it. Her daughter had signed her up but did not mention it to us, so we were in the dark. I began to laugh and laid the phone down on Brenda's vanity chair and went downstairs. As Mary talked with the owner of the restaurant, Brenda explained to me how she had filled out two slips for the raffle the week before while picking up a food order. Little did she imagine that Mary's name would be picked. As Mary continued to speak with the gentleman, I went back up to the bathroom to put the receiver back on the phone. As I entered the bathroom, there was Tiffany sitting on the chair listening intently to the conversation. "Well, young lady," I said, "Are you eavesdropping on Grandma?" Tiff looked up at me, meowed, and went right back to listening. Brenda and Mary laughed when I told them about our little busybody.

Tiffany and the Mice

Some years ago, Brenda and I came home from visiting one evening and were unwinding when Brenda looked down the hallway from the kitchen to the dining room. She remarked that Tiffany must have brought one of the catnip mice downstairs and was playing with it in the dining room. I came in from the back room and looked down the hallway just to see the "catnip" mouse run into the bathroom with Tiff right behind it. "Ah, Brenda," I called to my wife, "That's not a catnip mouse Tiffany has—it's a real one!" I quickly went to the bathroom and sure enough, it was a real, living, breathing, moving rodent. Genus: MUS, species: Musculus, mouse!

Tiffany looked up at me and meowed, obviously very proud

of herself, a cat with no front claws catching a mouse. I wasn't quite sure what to do next, but I knew I did not want my cat eating this yucky, dirty mouse. By this time, the little varmint was not too quick, having been mauled by his much larger opponent, so I put my foot on him just to make sure he would not get away. I called to Brenda to get my pliers and bring them to me. I then got a firm hold on Mr. Mouse and took him out back and disposed of him. I did not want him making a return visit. I was glad that it was Tiffany who caught the intruder and not Taffy. She would not have been so willing to give up her prey as was her more amicable sister.

The second episode with a mouse took place one night when we were home watching TV. We knew that Tiff was sleeping on the wooden rocking chair in the front living room, her favorite snoozing place downstairs. All of a sudden I saw a mouse scurry from the back room through the kitchen and down the hallway. I informed Brenda about my alien sighting and turned to our "supposed-to-be-alert-to-mice-in-the-house" kitty and exclaimed, "What a guard cat you are, Tiffany, the mice are walking away with the place." And with that we went back to watching TV, hoping the mouse would return to the back room and get caught in the trap we had set in the closet.

It must have been only 10 or 15 minutes later when Tiffany came trotting from the back room into the living room right past my chair into the front living room. I noticed her but was too engrossed in my TV program to see anything else. But Brenda did! "Clair! Tiffany has a mouse!" Both of us were up and out of our chairs in a flash. Sure enough, Tiffers had a little gray mouse. She looked pleased as punch (whatever that means), and she dropped it at my feet. Once more I placed my foot on the little critter so that it did not escape and told Brenda to get the pliers. Out the door it went, never to invade the confines of our home again.

We petted our little heroine, and she ate up the attention like she always does. I have never seen a cat like Tiffany who soaks up attention and affection like a furry sponge. She wants to be with us all the time—a real kitty cuddler.

Cats Glued to the Tube

A few years ago, Brenda and I were watching a Public Television program on cats, from England, I think. We had watched it for about 15 minutes when little Miss Tiffany strolled into the room. She was looking for an empty lap when the cats' meowing on the TV caught her attention. She stopped cold in her tracks and parked herself right in front of the set and watched the rest of the program—a total of 45 minutes. Our little feline was glued to the tube, watching intently as the cats played, hunted, fought, ate, slept, and meowed. The only time she lost interest or looked away was when some "human" took center stage and tried to dazzle her with his expertise on cats. Tiff did not seem impressed in the least.

Brenda thought quickly and taped most of the program on our VCR. She is the VCR expert in our household. Thanks to her I have 21 Audie Murphy movies in my archives. These are all taped from the American Movie Classics Channel without the annoying commercials. It is great when AMC shows movies like *Ben Hur, The Ten Commandments, The Robe, The Greatest Story Every Told, The Bible*, and other biblical films. You know, worthwhile stuff to watch.

So we saved the program on cats to show Taffy who was up-stairs napping at the time. Now the Taff is not as much a TV buff as Tiffany, but this program did catch and keep her attention. We enjoyed watching it again but had more fun watching Taffy and her reactions to the show. Like Tiff, she stayed for the entire 45 minutes, engrossed in all those cats.

Tiffany and Ichthammol

Most cats like catnip. Many cat owners have told me that their cats have informed them that if they give them catnip, they are not to be held responsible for their actions. The cat, that is! Well, our cats like catnip, not to eat, but to smell and nuzzle in a toy. Tiffany also licks the catnip pouches our neighbor Louise Evans gave them some time ago. In fact, she gets them soaked! And if we try to take one from her when she is licking, scratching, nuzzling, etc., she growls like a real mean kitty.

However, there is something else that puts Tiffers into more of a weird trance than catnip—Ichthammol! As a kid, I knew it as black salve, and my Mother used it many times to relieve the pain of cuts, scratches, burns, and other mishaps an overactive boy encounters while playing. In fact, Brenda and I still use it often due to the minor hazards we face in working around the parsonage.

It was because of one of these "battle scars" that we accidentally discovered our furball's obsession with the black stuff. Brenda incurred some injury and had put some Ichthammol on a finger and covered it with a band-aid. She went into the bedroom and petted Tiffany who was lying on the bed. Well, when Tiff got a whiff of the Ichthammol, she went after Brenda's hand, trying to nuzzle the cut finger. My poor wife wasn't quite sure what was going on at first until she noticed that Tiffany was after the one finger with the band-aid. She allowed the pussycat to rub and nuzzle her finger all the while noticing the look of ecstasy on her face.

Brenda couldn't wait to tell me about the incident and our feline's fascination with the black salve. Whenever we applied it to our hands or feet, little Miss Tiffany smelled it with her keen nose and ran to our side and began going through her routine. Once, Brenda purposely dropped the tube on the floor to see what the kitty would do. She smelled it, pushed it, laid down and held it between her paws and nuzzled it. She did everything but carry it away. Tiff still goes bonkers over the Ichthammol, but it has no effect upon Taffy whatsoever.

The Tooth

In July of 1995, during a regular check-up at the vets, Dr. Vance Case of the animal hospital, detected that Tiffany had infected gums. Upon further inspection, Dr. Case discovered a bad tooth which required extraction. Our little sweetie had to spend a day or two overnight at the hospital and take antibiotics when she came home. It is always fun to give a cat medicine, and the Tiffers did not like it one bit. However, she recovered fully and does not seem to miss the tooth.

Grandma Arrives

As I mentioned earlier in this chapter, Brenda's mother moved in with us and, of course, this caused some changes for us, including the cats. Her husband, Donald, had passed away a few months earlier. He had been in a nursing home in Lancaster, requiring skilled care. Mary was a resident of a personal care facility, needing some assistance but not full-time help. You can imagine the costs, and we knew that Mary could not continue to live in the Retirement Center. Her money would be gone in a couple of years. So I made the suggestion to Brenda that we offer our home to her, providing the churches had no problem with it, and if there were no insurance technicalities. Of course our loving people found no problem with the move and commended us for opening our hearts and our door to Mary.

This idea occurred to us some years before when Brenda's parents were contemplating a move due to health reasons. We also wanted them closer to us so that we could do more for them. We would rather have them dependent on us than someone else who perhaps would not give them the care and attention they needed and deserved.

So on Mary's 80th birthday, we went to Lancaster County and brought Mary to our humble home in Sunbury. Brenda's brother, Bill, rented a U-haul truck and brought Mary's few belongings that we fit neatly into the parsonage. Here, besides being with family who loves her, she would be surrounded with familiar furnishings—all the things that she and Don had given to us over the years.

We converted the dining room into a bedroom for Mary, purchased a bed and moved her antique chest of drawers, wash stand, and china closet into the room to make a cozy place for her. We added a night stand, used the lamps she had at the Retirement Center, and hung some pictures and knick-knacks to provide some semblance of days gone by. It's not the house on Reservoir Street in Lancaster, or even the huge apartment at Willow Valley, but she is satisfied and happy. That was our intent.

Now Tiffany was used to Mary, having stayed at her home and apartment when we visited the Barnetts on vacation. Tiff would come out to the living room where we were sitting and jump up on the couch with us and make herself right at home. She would get within touching distance of Mary and Don without any apparent concern. She was not afraid of them and seemed comfortable in their presence. In fact, one time when we attended a class reunion of Brenda's, Tiffany came out, jumped up on the back of the sofa and spent the evening with Grandma and Grandpa. She jumped down only when Brenda and I made a noise at the door, and she did not know it was us.

Brenda caught a glimpse of her jumping down and said to her mother, "We don't allow Tiffany to get up on the back of our good sofa at home. She shouldn't be up on yours. She still has her back claws and may also get cat hair on it."

Mary defended the kitty, "She wasn't hurting anything and besides we thought it was cute."

So Grandma overruled us right there and then, and Tiff was allowed on the back of the sofa. Brenda did, however, put a folded sheet over it to take some protective measures against pulls and hair. She is allowed the same leeway at Grammy and Grandpap Shaffers.' It's so hard to raise cats these days with the Grandparents spoiling them!

Well, Tiff was a little surprised to see Grandma at her house instead of at Lancaster. She had checked out the new furnishings in the converted dining room, and we had told her and Taffy that Grandma was coming. But still it was a little shock for our kitty to have Grandma come and not leave. Mary noticed Tiffany staring at her and said, "Look at the pussycat. She's wondering, 'What's she doing here? How long is she going to stay?'"

It did take Tiff a few days to get used to Mary's lift chair. Mommy and Daddy didn't have a chair like that. And even though she saw it in Lancaster, it was quite a different thing to see it in her living room. Like all of Grandma's belongings, it got the once-over. We are sure that at night both cats would sneak downstairs and check out the "smells" of our new boarder. Taffy would come stare in at Mary long after she had gone to bed.

Brenda and I have a bad habit at mealtime: We eat on snack trays in front of the TV. Our evening meal is consumed while we watch programs taped earlier on the VCR. Our "evening" meal is usually around 3:30-4:00 p.m. due to our visitation. We like to let our food digest properly, and we know that in most cases, our visits will involve some snacks. (That is probably the main reason for the early supper time. We'll admit it!)

Recently, Tiffany began to show up at lunch and supper time. Once, Brenda was eating some liverwurst, and Tiff was meowing and looking up at her. I finally said, "Give her a small piece on a napkin." My accommodating wife put a tiny sliver on a napkin and laid it down on the floor. Miss Tiffany gobbled it up and was back for more. So our kitty cat likes liverwurst! We did not give her any more at that time, but she seemed to think whenever Brenda was eating on her tray that Mommy had liverwurst.

Grandma added a new dimension, so to speak, to the cats' lives when she moved in with us—especially Tiffany's. Our little furball began sitting right in front of Grammy's chair, watching her intently as she ate. Mary would say to her, "What's the matter? Don't they feed you? Are you hungry?"

At first, Tiff made no vocal response, but gradually she answered Mary nearly every time she spoke to her. Mary also would "offer" the kitty whatever she was eating and usually our little gray and white "Moocher" would wrinkle her nose and back away. Brenda would again explain to her mother that this cat had the best food money could buy and that we did not give her scraps from the table, except, of course, an occasional morsel of liverwurst and a taste of vanilla ice milk. Mary came back with, "But she looks so hungry!"

Brenda tried to reassure her, "Mother! That little scrounge is not hungry! She is only being a pest. She just wants something different."

Grandma persisted, "Well, it won't hurt to give her a bite."

My wife looked at me. "I give up!"

Tiffany does not mind getting close to Mary as she sits on a small footstool at the window next to her lift chair and allows her to pass by on the wheelchair within a few inches or so. She still sits or lays nearby and watches Mary for long periods of time. We all wonder just what is going on in that little mind. Cats are great for staring at you for what seems forever sometimes. My wife and I agree that Tiffany seems very happy that Grandma has come to stay with us. So are we.

Chapter 11

Taffy, Taffy, Taffy!

Dr. George Salzmann, our veterinarian, said it: "Taffy, Taffy, Taffy!" during a checkup following a near crisis with our beloved multi-colored kitty. I will talk about this later in this chapter. After Dr. Salzmann's remark, we all laughed knowing the implication about little "Miss Mind-of-her-Own."

Taffy is hard to win over. Compared to Tiffany, she is a challenge. Cooperation is not her strong suit. Both cats dislike going to the animal hospital; most pets do. They think the vet is their destination as soon as they are put in the pet taxi. When we walk in the door, the smell confirms it. Their anxiety heightens immediately, and we talk to them softly trying to assure them that it is okay.

Dr. Salzmann is not only a veterinarian, he is a cat lover, or perhaps we should say, an animal lover. He has a gift with animals, and they seem to know it. Taffy was no exception. She sensed his concern and compassion, and although she was frightened, she calmed down and was unusually content as Dr. Salzmann examined her. We appreciated his ability to make our traumatized tabby more comfortable and serene under the circumstances. We kid the good folks at the animal hospital by saying that Taffy "asks" for Dr. Salzmann by name.

Extra TLC

If you read the chapter on the Big Cat Spat with any serious attention at all, you are aware that we tread carefully around Taffy. After she "flipped out" on us a couple of times, we changed our whole approach to this cat. When there is a confrontation between T and T, we do not get excited now, nor do we lose our cool. We simply ask, "Is everybody okay? Is Tissy, Tassy okay?" This usually settles any problems before they develop into something serious. We do not want a repeat of the cat spat!

When we handle Taffers to give her medications or clean her ears and eyes or just check her over, we always talk softly and reassuringly to her. She is so much more easily traumatized that Tiffany. It is the same when we have to transport her somewhere. We get the pet taxi ready as quietly as possible and take it to where Taffy is sleeping or cat-napping. We pick her up, all the while speaking baby talk to her, and very gently place her in the carrier. She is still nervous, of course, but the extra TLC helps and, so far, it has worked.

A Favorite Spot

Ever since Taffy was a kitten, one of her favorite places to be is smack dab in the middle of my desk. This is, of course, when I am sitting there trying to study or work. In chapter two I told how Brenda brought Smokey in and up to my study and plopped her on my desk. Smokey loved it and, like her Aunt, Taffy carries on the tradition.

It certainly is one way for her to get my undivided attention. When she is laying in the middle of my desk, I can't do my work. How can I ignore this precious pussycat who is purring up a storm and looking at me with dreamy eyes? The little squirt seems to know that she can melt us with her cat charm, and we cannot resist petting and loving her.

As a kitten, Taffy used to go after things on my desk such

as pens, paper clips, erasers, and the like, and push them off the edge onto the floor. Then, she would look down at them and at me as if to say, "Oops!" However, after I would pick them up and put them back on the desk, her remorse was short-lived. Off they would go again. Of course I was very careful to keep track of all the small items and not allow Taffy to get them into her mouth. Taff is notorious for going after tiny items, much more so than Tiff, and we have to be on the alert all the time.

A Favorite Pastime

Some years ago, Taffers began coming into the bathroom when I was taking my morning shower. If I would shut the door, which I normally did to eliminate noise because Brenda was still sleeping, Taff would meow and push on the door creating a loud fuss. Had I already gotten into the shower and did not hear her at the door, Mommy would get up, come over, and let the persistent puddy cat in. I finally decided to let the door ajar to prevent the annoying thumping so my wife's sleep would not be interrupted. In the colder months we use a small heater rather than turn up the furnace and it works well, warming up the bathroom. Unless, that is, said pussycat kicks the door wide open letting the cold air in while I am in the shower. So far we haven't been able to train her to close the door. Cats do not like closed doors, so why would Taffy want to close it?

My patient, well, somewhat patient little buddy, waited until I got out of the shower and then let me know she wanted some attention. The meowing got so loud that Brenda came over to see what I was doing to the cat. This was when the thing first began. Of course I protested vigorously that I was not harming the pussycat, but that she wanted my undivided attention. This satisfied my concerned spouse, and she went back to bed.

I got down on the floor and petted my furry little friend

who was purring profusely and meowing at the same time. We get a kick out of it when they do this because it alters the meow, and it sounds neat. Often when our two do it, especially Taffy, it sounds like a bark. We call them puppercats and pussydogs because they often act more like dogs than cats. They act like people, too, but more about that later. We have found, also, that cats feel safer if their humans are down on their level. Our size intimidates them.

As I was petting Taffy on the bathroom floor, she came up to my head and sniffed my wet hair. Then she licked it, chewed on it, nuzzled it, laid on it, and kneaded it. This process has been repeated just about every time I wash my hair, not necessarily in the order above. She thinks I just have to let her do this. Whenever I get out of the shower and do not wash my hair, she looks at me with what I am sure is a disappointed expression and usually wants out of the bathroom.

If Brenda hears Taffy pawing at the door and me letting her out, she often calls over from the bedroom and says, "Does the kitty want out? Is she giving Daddy the brush off?"

I answer, "Yes, I didn't get down on the floor with her so your persnickety pussycat wanted out!" I know how I rate!

Just why Taffy enjoys nuzzling my wet hair—actually even laying her whole body on my head—I am not sure. Perhaps it is something carried over from kittenhood while she was in the moist, protective womb, I don't know. Maybe it is from a maternal instinct placed in her by our Creator God, and although Taffy has not and will not have kittens, the instinct to care for babies is there. Who knows? In any event, she seems to love this routine, and when I am able, I accommodate our little feline friend.

Sleeping With Mommy

Our cats are comfortable with either of us and will accept affection and spend time with us both. From the beginning, if one of us had an available lap they were on it. Sure, they like their privacy at times, but most of the time they want to be with us, no doubt because of all the attention we have given them. Animals, like people, respond to love and consideration.

Another routine Taffy developed years ago was catnapping with Brenda during the afternoon. Brenda had quit her job with the drug company for which she had worked for 13 years prior to our move to the parsonage. This freed her to do things at the house and develop other interests. Even when she took on a part-time job, she still had afternoons free. When the kitties came along, it did not take long for the close relationships we have with them to form. Cats, especially, like routine and structure. Our two know that Sunday mornings mean a small treat of canned tuna. Like clockwork they are in the kitchen letting us know they want their dish of fish! How they know it's Sunday, I have no idea, but they do!

When Brenda worked full time for a three-year span at the chicken plant, Taffy missed her afternoon rendezvous with Mommy, and she did not like it one bit. At first she gave Brenda a cold shoulder, but then finally mellowed as Mommy went out of her way to win her kitty's affection. Taff seemed to adjust to the new schedule but was really happy when the job ended and the afternoon routine resumed.

The actual napping is comical because our multi-colored pussycat has her own ideas as to how a nap should be conducted. Taffy jumps up at the head of the bed, sometimes startling you but often so gracefully that she cannot be detected at this point. Her next move is to circle Brenda, going from the head to the foot at least once and perhaps several times. We think she must be part Indian, you know, circling the wagons? If Mommy does not acknowledge her presence immediately, the next step is to breathe into her face. This method is sometimes accompanied by loud purring. Didn't work! No response from the snoozing human. Okay, plan three: paw at Mommy's arm, knead it if necessary. If there is still no movement from Brenda, more drastic measures are taken. Step four involves backing up to her face and swishing the tail, of course right in Mommy's face. Very often this works, but if it doesn't, number five calls for nuzzling the hair. Still no response? Okay, "Mommy Dearest, you asked for it!" Plan six: crawl on top of her! This almost always gets results. Mommy wakes up, or gives in, and pets the persistent pussycat who now has snuggled tightly up against her. She is now content; let the nap begin!

Oh, yes, one other method Taffy will resort to is to purr profusely, form slobber in her mouth, and then shake it off, in Mommy's face! Guaranteed results! The tissue box is nearby, so my wet wife can dry herself off.

Sleeping with Mommy is not confined to the afternoon. Taffy will sleep with us at night, on Brenda's side, either right beside her or at the top of her pillow, or should I say "pillows." My spouse sleeps with four pillows, three regular size and one body pillow. The kitty has no problem finding a pillow to curl up on. She usually does not stay the whole night especially if I am in the bed, too. Brenda and I shift around a lot and this disturbs Taffy, who, when settled in, does not want to be disturbed.

Another cute sidelight to Taffy's sleeping with Mommy routine is when I get up in the morning. If the kitty has been napping somewhere else, she often waits until I go into the bathroom or for a walk, and then scurries over to the bedroom and hops in with Brenda. I come back to find her stretched out beside my "better-half" with a look of "I got Mommy all to myself." It could give a guy a complex.

Caper of the Christmas Ribbon

During one Christmas season, I was busy wrapping gifts in my study when little Miss Multi-colored Kitty waltzed in, no doubt intrigued by the sound of wrinkling paper. She could have just been being nosy or wanting attention, but in any event, she graced me with her presence. Now I am not known for my gift wrapping ability, but this was one of those years I was trying to be fancy. I had some ribbon and was snipping off ends, and a few pieces fell on the floor. Having noticed Taffy come in and knowing her history with such things, I quickly bent down to pick up the ribbon. I wasn't fast enough; Taff had a piece and was heading for the door. I pursued, calling to her to drop the ribbon. Fat chance! The little squirt trotted into the spare bedroom and under the crib. I shooshed her out, making sure she still had the piece of ribbon in her mouth. From there she scooted down the stairs and into the living room and behind the sofa. I was able to get her out from behind that refuge, and she ran back up the steps. I followed, trying to convince my pussycat to give up the ribbon. This time she headed under the bed. I shut the door and crawled after the little culprit.

By this time, Brenda, who had been downstairs on orders not to come into my study, was wondering just exactly what was going on. "Why are you chasing my cat?" she shouted through the closed door, as I lay prone on my stomach under the bed attempting to get the ribbon from Taffy.

"She ran off with a piece of ribbon," I answered her question. But after cornering the fleeing feline under the bed, I could not find any ribbon. We did not find any trace of it in the house anywhere so we could only assume that she ate it. However, it never showed up in the litter box so just what did happen to it remains an unsolved mystery. And my wife likes telling about this hilarious scene of her husband chasing a poor little kitty cat through the house trying to extract a tiny piece of Christmas ribbon from her grasp. The moral of the story, if there is one, is that I rarely use ribbon anymore, and if I do, I am very careful with it.

"Taffy, Don't Look at Me That Way"

Certain people can look at you and seemingly look right through you and cause you to feel very uneasy. One of my fine parishioners, Clara Boone, often said that her father just had to glance at her and her brothers and sisters without saying a word when her mother told them to do something. No words were necessary—the look did the trick. My dad had that same "look." When I was the recipient of his glare, I knew what would soon follow if I did not listen.

Our little feline has an uncanny way of staring at us that intrigues our imagination, making us wonder just what it is that she's thinking. One morning several years ago, I was in my study talking with Mollie Raker on the phone about some church business, when I noticed Taffy come up the steps and sit at the top of the stairs. Mollie, one of the hard-working ladies in our St. Elias Church, and yours truly talked for about 45 minutes. The whole time little Miss Taffy sat in the same spot and stared at me during the conversation. To my knowledge, she never once took her eyes off me for the entire 45 minutes. It was eerie. I told Mollie about this as we were ready to hang up, and she was surprised that Taffers would sit there so long. It was not to be an isolated incident.

Brenda and I were in bed one morning, about to get up, and I happened to look down the hallway. Right outside the spare bedroom door sat the multi-colored kitty...staring! We waited a while, took a few extra winks, and lo and behold, the pussycat was still there staring at us. This has happened many times over the years, at various times of the day.

One night after we retired to bed, my wife and I were talking and she said, "I wonder where you-know-who is?" I answered, "I have an idea. Sit up and look down the hallway." I quietly picked up the flashlight on my table next to the bed and shined it down the hallway. Right inside the spare bedroom was the kitty, once again staring intently.

"What is she looking at?" I whispered to Brenda.

"Us," she replied softly.

"I know that," I whispered, "but why?"

"I don't know...I'm not a cat," offered my wise-cracking

spouse. This nightly routine has been repeated over and over down through the years as our feline never seems to grow weary of "watching."

Cat experts seem to think that our furry friends are observing us, perhaps intrigued by these creatures known as humans. They are curious, we know this, and just maybe, with their limited power of reason, they are trying to come to some understanding of these interesting and odd-acting critters called people. We know that they are very intelligent and perceptive just by observing them. I have watched my cats and other cats outside work out problems, whether in getting to food, playing with a toy, or hunting prey. They can think and reason to some degree.

Taffy and Grandma

Unlike her sister, Taffy has not accepted Grandma's presence in our home. Apparently she sees Mary as an intruder who has invaded her domain and is also a threat to her well-being. Tiffy pretty easily accepted our new resident, deciding that Mary is not here to harm her and so she will make the best of it. Tiff is an adapter or adjuster to a situation, like a little furry optimist who weighs the possibilities and takes advantage of the opportunities. We all can learn from the Tiffers.

Taffy, however, is not so optimistic. She seems to survey every situation and see only the negative side of things. Although she is the toughest physically of the two cats, she is not tough psychologically. Taff is more spooky, being easily frightened by a noise or a voice she may not immediately recognize. Her philosophy is "caution first"—run and hide and then check out the situation later. To some people that may seem like a good rule to follow, but avoiding problems, people, or situations doesn't solve anything. The positive, creative approach is the constructive method of dealing with any unpleasantness. So far, I haven't been able to convince my multi-colored pal of that.

Since Grandma moved in, Taffy has confined her trips downstairs to early morning before Grandma rises, or late at night after she has retired. Sometimes she does come down when Mary is in her chair and as long as no one makes a sudden move, she will stay in the hallway or the kitchen, at least for a while. We suspect that she does some exploring or investigating during the wee hours of the night when all of us are in bed. We used to shut the kitties upstairs at night to prevent any problems that might arise, but with Mary downstairs we are confident about allowing them to roam wherever they wish. So far it has worked. Her presence seems to be like a guard on duty. They know she is there, and their behavior has been exemplary.

Grandma has talked to Taffy as she does to Tiffany, but this seems to be a signal to the kitty to exit the party. We began kidding around and saying things like, "Taffy has left the building." We coax, we plead, we try to convince her everything is okay, and we won't give up.

The Kitty Was All Wired Up

One afternoon, I came home from visiting and found Brenda taking a nap in our bedroom. I decided to join her for about 20 minutes before supper and laid down beside her. I don't remember if we solicited Taffy's presence, but it wasn't too long before she jumped up with us and went through her usual routine. She finally parked herself beside Brenda and, of course, wanted to be petted. My wife accommodated her and began stroking and petting the felicitous feline.

As Brenda continued to stroke Taffy, the kitty raised up her rear end and Brenda felt a stiff protrusion under her tail. Upon closer observation, she saw that it was wire-like and was protruding from Taffy's rectum. She called my attention to it, and we both tried to examine it and carefully remove it. Our efforts did not seem to bother Taffy or cause her any discomfort. However, we quickly decided that a trip to the vet was in order. The object would not budge.

We explained the situation and the receptionist instructed us to come right over. We gratefully hurried our precious pussycat into a pet taxi and to the hospital.

Dr. Salzmann made a preliminary examination and asked some questions and then called for x-rays. He told us to go home and call back in an hour or so. We returned to the house in some anticipation and concern. Taffy did not appear to be in any pain, but since they can't really tell you, we couldn't really know.

About 45 minutes later the phone rang. It was Dr. Salzmann.

"Clair, when did this cat last have a bowel movement?"

"Well, Dr. Salzmann, I'm not really sure since we have two cats and two litter boxes."

"Well, Taffy was filled up with stools. She couldn't have a bowel movement. We sedated her and dilated her rectum to remove the stools. They were hard, like rocks. What kind of cat food do you feed them?"

"We keep Science Diet Lite hard food down for them all the time. And we give them some soft food as a treat and some canned tuna every day."

"Cut out the soft food altogether and limit the canned food to twice a week. The soft cat food has a tendency to bind some cats up. I would eliminate it altogether. We are not sure what this wire is that was sticking out of Taffy. The reason you could not pull it out was because it was imbedded in a stool. We would like to keep her overnight and you may pick her up tomorrow. She is quite sedated now anyway."

After seeing the x-rays the next day, we thanked the Lord that Brenda spotted the piece of wire protruding from Taffy. As it turned out, it was not wire, but elastic used in reupholstering. That made sense since we have several overstuffed chairs in the house. At first, Dr. Salzmann questioned us about fishing equipment, thinking perhaps that Taff had swallowed a hook with some line on it. I assured him that there was nothing like that in the house since I am not a fisherman (except as a minister I am a "fisher of men").

We found some of the same type of elastic that Taffy swallowed on the bottom of one of our recliners. It was all intact and the piece that our little furball found must have been a loose end. Leave it to the Taffers! She has a knack for discovering such things.

Dr. Salzmann also recommended giving our cats Laxatone, a laxative and lubricant to help remove hair balls, at least twice a week. We put some on a front paw two times a week, and things have gone well so far. He also prescribed a new higher fiber hard cat food for our felines, and they have taken to it just fine. Taffy has had no problems in the litter box.

Needless to say, we keep an even closer eye on our two furry friends since we love and appreciate them so much. We know that they love us, too, and we want the best for them that we can possibly provide. They depend upon us to take care of them and to be aware and alert when something is wrong. This takes some time and some effort, but they are well worth it.

Parents have been given by God an even greater responsibility to care for their children. It is unfortunate today, when so many are quick to claim child abuse, that we see parents terrified to discipline their children. The result is unstructured, undisciplined and permissive personalities emerging from the children. An absence of respect for people, their possessions and rights has led to downright discourtesy, disorder, discrimination, and rampant crime. All in all, the result has been a real breakdown in the value and worth of human life. As we continue to restrict parents, hobble our law enforcement officials, promote immorality, legalize abortions on demand, and turn our backs on God, the situation will get worse. I love America, and I hate to see her disintegrating from within by the irresponsible actions of those who care little for the spiritual values upon which she became great. God has been patient with us and so very good to us. How long can we continue to presume upon His kindness? We must return to spiritual values and use the Bible as the rule for our way of life.

Chapter 12

Sammy!

In the spring, our neighbor, Barbara Shipman, took a walk up the road next to our home. We refer to this road as "the hollow" because it winds up the mountain surrounded by trees over both sides, making it somewhat dark. It is an eerie stroll up this road at night.

As Barb began walking back down the hollow, she heard a meow and turned to see a jet black kitten running after her. The little tyke must have been hiding in the field along the road and when she saw Barb, she ran out to see if any relationship could be established. Apparently, she was the sad victim of a "drop off"—another unwanted pet. But this kitten was persistent, and she knew that she liked Barb right away.

Now Barb and her husband Bill have ample cats on their farm to keep the barn and the surrounding buildings and grounds somewhat free of pests. They didn't really need another cat. But there seemed to be something special about this little critter, something none of us could explain.

Well, the little squirt adopted our neighborhood immediately and made herself right at home. And we fell in love with her almost from the start. She slept on Louise's back porch most of the time, but once in a while we would find her curled up on ours. She became a community cat.

The New Kitty Is Named

Between our three families—the Evans, the Shipmans, and us—we usually come up with names for the outside cats. I suggested "Little Black Sambo" but Louise cautioned that it might not be "ethnically correct." I had a viewmaster when I was a youngster, and one of my discs was the story of Little Black Sambo.

Now I was raised not to be prejudiced against anyone, and I have followed that teaching all my life. As a minister, I preach and teach that all people are created by God equally and that no race is superior or inferior. However, we did like the name Sambo but finally settled on Sammy.

Then my fun-loving wife began calling the little kitty "Samantha Louise" as even our resisting neighbor was quite taken with Sammy. Louise was up to this new development, however, and quickly pointed out that the kitten could be named after Brenda as well, since her middle name was Louise. It became a cute contest as Brenda and Louise both insisted that Sammy was the other's namesake.

Little Melter of Human Hearts

Sammy was much like our Tiffany—wherever you were, that is where she wanted to be. She followed Louise from one place to another, insisting on being right in the thick of things. If Louise was sitting down working in her garden or flower bed, Sammy did her best to get on her lap. If Louise was standing, Sammy often tried to crawl up her leg, or she would lay nearby hoping that Louise would sit down and make her lap accessible. We chuckled as we watched this little love bug follow Louise everywhere she went.

If Louise was not available, anyone was fair game for Samantha, but it was usually Brenda whom Sammy found! In fact, after a while, the two ladies attempted to pawn the pussycat off on each other. Louise would say, "Okay, Sammy, go see what Brenda is doing." Or she would bring the kitty to Brenda and say, "It's your turn to babysit the little pest." Brenda did the same thing, and they both did it to Barb. Sammy didn't seem to mind, and she accommodated herself to whomever was available. Barb's daughters, Jen and Jo, also were smitten by Sammy's charm. When they could, they spent some time with her. Everyone was her friend.

As I said before, Louise was not particularly a cat lover, but she made allowances for this special little kitty. One day when she was eating lunch on her back porch, I meandered over for some reason and lo and behold, Sammy was on her lap. A "cat" was on Louise's lap—while she was eating lunch no less! This was too good to keep! Louise had not seen me approach so I scurried back to get Brenda for this unheard of phenomenon. We came back over and confronted our diminutive neighbor with how and why this "cat" was on her lap. As I remember, Louise was not sure just how Sammy got there, but since she was there, she might as well stay. Suffice it to say, this became a regular occurrence. Sammy was winning a reluctant cat lover over.

I must admit that I, too, was quite taken with our new furry friend. Whenever I came out the back door and she heard me, she came running. She followed me up to the garage and all around the yard—my little "black shadow." In the garage, she would explore and get all dusty and covered with cobwebs, or jump up on the workbench and watch me work. She was the "purrfect" little companion. I must say that if we did not already have Taff and Tiff as house cats, I would have taken Sammy inside in a minute. This adorable little gregarious feline stole my heart.

Feisty Feline

Sammy was playful like all kittens are, but she loved to surprise you. The little imp would hide behind something and come flying out at you without warning. If you were not quick enough, she would land on your leg and dig her claws in to hold on. Most of us decided that she was just "feisty."

Feisty may have been a mild word to describe Sammy. We began to play with her in the yard and sometimes would roll her over on her back. If she thought we were getting too rough or getting the best of her, she would growl and scratch and bite and come after us with a vengeance. The little kitty had a temper. Often I would hear Brenda say, "You little monster!" Then she would retreat to the house for some rubbing alcohol to dab on the scratches.

Cats were not exempt from Sammy's surprise attacks. She was not afraid of the other outside cats even if they were three times her size. If she wanted to play, she went after them. No amount of growling, hissing, hair-raising, or cuffing deterred this determined kitten. The cats usually ran away from her and found some place to hide until she settled down. If they made her angry enough, she would follow after them, swiping at them with her little paws. She did find one black and white male who loved to play with her, and they played together marvelously until he was hit by a car. If any of us were around during the day, we tried to monitor her whereabouts to keep her from going near the road. However, we all knew we could not keep an eye on an outside cat 24 hours a day.

Sammy Worms Her Way In

Neither Louise nor Bill and Barb have indoor pets. Louise and Bill definitely do not want any in the house, and Barb probably could be persuaded, if daughters Jen and Jo had their way. Both girls grew attached to Sammy. Their son Jim was not so amicable toward the little feisty cat who once got in his shiny new car. All nine lives were severely threatened as a result of that incident.

However, when Bill and Jim were away, somehow Sammy showed up inside the Shipman house. She was seen sleeping on a couch or chair, being carried about by female admirers, or just scampering around at will. I am not sure if Bill and Jim found out right away, although I do know they were aware of it later. Bill may have greatly protested, but I suspect that this little furball was tugging on his heart strings, too.

Brenda and I were reluctant to let Sammy in our back room because of fleas or other pests known to cling to outdoor cats, and also because her scent would upset Taff and Tiff. It was very tempting to let her in to have a special treat away from the other cats and to play with her, but we resisted.

Sammy followed Barb and Louise over to Louise's other house on the opposite side of the parsonage. They were doing some work on the house, and the little squirt had to investigate the new territory. Several times Brenda and I moseyed over to see how things were coming along, and lo and behold, there was Samantha curled up on a piece of furniture taking a nap or prowling about the premises. We took note that this little pussycat was being granted some special privileges. It was hard not to "give in" to her. As I said before, she was just special.

One morning as I was taking some letters to our mailbox, I paused on the front porch to watch a cute sight. Louise was putting some flowers out for Barb on her flower stand along the road. Barb makes up flower arrangements to sell and does quite nicely. It is on an honor system, and most people are happy to cooperate. Apparently Louise had tried to sneak away from Sammy, but the little monster had followed her and was right there with Louise along busy Route 890. She attempted to chase Sammy back up to the house but to no avail. Sammy would run the opposite way and had Louise frantic. I was about to run to Louise's rescue when her sister, Sarah, came from the house and scooped Sammy up in her arms and held her until Louise was finished. I couldn't wait for Brenda to come home and relate this newest episode to her about our re-luctant cat lover neighbor. It was just too good to keep. Sammy even wormed her way into the hearts of those who came to visit any of the three families.

It was difficult not to adore this black, green-eyed little spitfire. She just seemed to have that type of personality that people are drawn to. Sammy loved life, and she expected it to love her back. I'm glad that this little creature of God came into our lives and touched us with her enthusiasm and zest for living. We learned from our feline friend that we should keep looking for the joy in life and major on that, not the negatives which are depressing and confusing. Everyone should be on the lookout for the lessons God has for us in the least likely places, like a little cat.

Thank You, Lord, for Sammy

I wish I could say that Sammy's story has a happy ending, and that she is still with us. However, reality is not like fiction in which we can write our own scenario and control what happens. In this real life story we could not control the script; we could not protect our little friend.

We don't know what happened to Sammy. One afternoon we noticed her along the road in front of our house, just lying in the grass motionless. Brenda went right to her and knew immediately Sammy was in trouble. I cautioned her, as she examined the kitten, that injured animals often strike out against people trying to help them due to pain and trauma. Not Sammy! Not this little sweetie. She just licked Brenda's hand and tried to respond and show her appreciation.

My loving wife carefully picked Sammy up in a towel and noticed that she cried when her abdomen was touched. We took her into our back room and laid her on the couch. Sammy hardly moved and just seemed very sick. We knew we could not keep her there and after consulting with our neighbor, Barb Shipman, we put her in their nice basement. We tried to make her as comfortable as possible but knew we were unable to help her. I never felt so helpless in my life.

We checked on Sammy the next morning, but her condition had not improved. All of us were worried and felt terrible about Sammy's suffering. Early that evening I checked on her again and Barb showed us a spot where she had passed some blood. I couldn't stand it any longer. Although we really could not afford it, I decided to call the vet. Bill and Barb agreed, and their daughter, Jo, went with us.

We put Sammy in a big file box and took her to our animal hospital hoping for some good news. Dr. Beverly Shaw did not hold out too much hope to us, however, diagnosing Sammy with some kind of internal injuries. How much money were we willing to spend on an outdoor cat that might not live through exploratory surgery, or if she did, might be hurt again or killed? We decided to have the veterinarian give her antibiotics and a pain killer and keep her overnight. I guess that made us feel better and soothed our consciences a bit. We left the hospital knowing that we probably had waited too long. Bill told us to put the cost on his farm account that he had with the animal hospital, but I declined since it was my idea and I felt better if we paid it. However, it ended up with Bill and Barb and Louise paying most of it and Brenda and I only a fraction. That's the kind of neighbors we have. We are so blessed to live next to them, and we know that God directed us here.

The next morning I reluctantly called over to the hospital to check on Sammy, and the lady I spoke with told me she would have one of the doctors call me. A little while later Dr. James Temple called us and very compassionately informed us that Sammy did not survive. After a few tears and hugs, we made arrangements to pick up our little friend. Dr. Temple said that the hospital would handle any "burial" arrangements for us, but we wanted to lay Sammy to rest ourselves.

I dug a deep hole in Brenda's flower bed near the old farm wagon in the back yard and used a metal file box for her coffin. We wrapped Sammy in a plastic bag and also wrapped the file box in a plastic leaf bag. Brenda placed some plastic flowers on her grave so we would know where it is.

A few days later, we received a sympathy card from the nice people at the animal hospital. It was a kind gesture on their part to express their understanding of our grief. Just a little stray cat, but we would miss her.

What did we learn from Sammy? For starters, I would say love, friendship, and trust. All three of those can get you hurt, and in Sammy's case, perhaps killed. As I mentioned before, she thought every human being was her friend. In fact, I think this little kitty saw every living creature as a pal. In a feline way, she loved life and expected life to love her back. I would hate to think that some mean-spirited person willfully hurt Sammy, but I know there are people out there like that. These individuals have a problem and desperately need our prayers. God help them and forgive them—that's my petition.

So because love, friendship and trust can lead to injury, do we stop loving, stop being friendly, stop trusting? No, I'll still side with Sammy because those things are Christ-like, and this poor world needs them in mega measure. Sure, you can get hurt when you lead with your heart, but it's worth it. Our Lord Jesus did. He made Himself vulnerable for our sakes and exposed His heart to friend and foe alike. On the cross, He bared His precious and perfect heart one final time, and someone rammed a spear through it. Would He do it again if His Father asked Him and if our salvation depended on it? You bet! So I will keep on loving, keep on making friends, and keep on trusting, even if it means experiencing a cross!

Thank you, Sammy, for reminding me and even showing me up from time to time. And thank you, Lord, for sending little Sammy our way. We got the message!

Chapter 13

Let the Animals Teach You

"But inquire of the animals, and they will instruct you," advises Job 12:7. It's a quaint thought to seek instruction from the animals. However, it is wise counsel from God's Word to a sometimes arrogant and presumptuous humanity which often misses the point its Creator is trying to make. We humans lose sight of the meaning and purpose of life in our high-tech and sophisticated world, and need the simplicity of "lesser" beings to right us and guide us back to what is true and worthwhile.

Some time ago, someone made the statement that life has no intrinsic meaning, and it is only what you bring into life and put into life that gives it meaning. I can agree with the philosophy that you get out of life what you put into it. That is true of anything, even the Christian faith. And, I can agree with the statement that life has no intrinsic meaning—without God! Apart from Him life has no meaning or purpose no matter how well-lived or philanthropic. He has designed life to be lived in a union with Him and for Him. If it is not, then something is missing, and it matters little in the end how successful or benevolent a person has been. It is when we find God—or He finds us—that the puzzle, the riddle, the confusion of life all starts to make sense. Sure, in this present existence we will not discover all the answers or understand everything. Our wise God knows that and does not expect us to. He simply asks us to believe and receive, to believe His Word as set forth in the Bible and to receive His Son, Jesus Christ, into our hearts and lives by faith. The Apostle Paul told the Philippian jailer, "Put your faith in the Lord Jesus, and you will be saved" (Acts 16:31). This is how we become actual children of God, by believing what God has said about His only Son, and appropriating the Lord Jesus' sacrifice on the cross for our sins by asking Him in faith to save our souls, to come in, take over, and manage our lives. Salvation, new birth, conversion—whatever we wish to call it—is a supernatural operation of God, who is Spirit, upon our human spirits, which changes us into new people with higher values, ideals, morals, and positive attitudes about life and each other.

Christians Are Like Cats

This statement is not original with me. I wish I could say that I thought of it all by myself, but I must attribute it to Dr. Stuart Lease who served for many years as President of Lancaster Bible College. In one of his classes, Dr. Lease was talking about Christians committing sins and what they should and need to do about it when it happens. In alluding to confession, Dr. Lease used the illustration of a cat. "Christians are like cats," he said, "or at least they should be. What does a cat do when he gets dirty? He goes somewhere secluded and cleans himself up. Isn't that what a Christian should do when he gets dirty, i.e., sins? Go somewhere alone with God and get cleaned up?"

The point is well taken: When a child of God sins, soils himself with some violation of God's Law, he immediately needs to confess it to his heavenly Father and receive forgiveness and cleansing: the sooner the better. One old preacher used to say, "Keep short accounts with God." In other words, don't let a sin linger: confess it and put it behind you. John the Apostle explains this in 1 John 1:9, "If we confess our sins, He is faithful and righteous and will forgive us our sins and cleanse us from all unrighteousness." The cleansing agent He uses is His Son's own blood (1 John 1:7).

Interestingly, the word "confess" in the Greek language of the New Testament is a combination of two words, *homo* and *lego*. *Homo*, of course, means "same"; *lego* means "to say." When we confess our sins to God we are "Saying the same thing" about them that He does. In other words, we are agreeing with God that our sins are wrong, that we have been disobedient, that we have hurt Him, ourselves, and others. Sin is destructive, and that is why we must take care of it immediately. Confession is the way.

So what does this have to with cats and their cleaning of themselves when dirty in particular? Simply this: A cat normally does not like to be dirty. Most do not care to be wet—ours don't. Like most of their feline relatives, they wash after a meal. If a cat does not keep itself clean, usually something is wrong with it. Isn't this similar to a Christian? He or she does not like being dirty, i.e., stained with sin. Hence, the clean up or confession. But if a Christian keeps getting dirty, with more than the normal day to day slip-ups, then something is wrong. The reasons could be many and complicated. Is he caught or trapped in a situation or impure relationship? Is he having difficulty living the Christian life? Are "well-meaning" believers imposing unrealistic demands upon him, thus causing him to become discouraged and confused? Is he angry for some reason with God, with people, with himself, and therefore in a state of rebellion? Is he sick? (This could be physical, mental, or emotional.) Of course, all human sin and problems are linked to "spiritual sickness" due to man's original transgression (see Genesis 3:1-24). The spiritual life of a "sick" Christian should be investigated first, but carefully, cautiously, and compassionately.

When our cats are off the beam, displaying unusual or unacceptable behavior, we know something is amiss. We have learned not to become upset with them or scold them; we rather try to understand what has happened and why they are acting this way. If we cannot locate the cause or the problem, we seek professional help at our local animal hospital. We love our two kitty companions and will go to great lengths to secure their well-being. Should we Christians not do the same with an errant brother or sister in the Lord? Are they not worth more than cats? They need patience, love, empathy, support, and time. There is no excuse for a callous, impatient, and abrasive approach to a troubled Christian. Such believers have problems themselves which need to be addressed.

So whether cats or Christians, tread carefully, lovingly, looking for the real problem so that pets or people can be what God intended them to be. If you can't do it with TLC, do not know how, or won't, then do them a favor. Get out of the way, and let someone who can and will do the job. And please, step aside quietly.

Without being too fanciful, I would now like to continue the comparison with cats and Christians, looking at some negative and some positive characteristics common to both. Christian cat lovers especially may appreciate the analogies and praise God for the lessons He teaches us in the most unlikely places.

Negative Characteristics

CURIOSITY: We all have heard the old saying, "Curiosity killed the cat." It's true that cats are very curious creatures, and this trait has led to the demise of many a feline, pet or stray. It seems that they just have to see what is on the other side of the road. Their hunting and investigative instincts drive them to cross that road, go into that farmer's field, barn, or shed, jump through the open window, squeeze through a slightly ajar door, crawl up near a warm car engine, and the list goes on. Although many of them have become "street smart" and have managed to live long lives as outdoor cats, most do not acquire those survival skills soon enough. The "nine lives" mystique seems to have passed them over.

As I reminisce about the cats we have had the pleasure to know over the years—those outdoor friends who graced our backyard and porch—I have to say that most of them had short lives. There was Smokey, Charcoal, Tyco, Coco, Pewter, Tigger, Fluffy, and of course, Sammy. Most of them did not make it to their first birthday. There are just too many hazards out there in this cold, cruel world, and we humans are responsible for our share of them. The automobile has to rank near the top on the list of "cat killers." Poison, guns, spoiled or contaminated food, predators, and even other cats are also on the list.

Cats are curious, and this often has been a characteristic that has led to their demise. True, perhaps their curiosity has been beneficial in many cases, and in regard to our two furballs, it has often been cute. We have watched them sneak up on something new we added to the house, sniff our clothes after we return home, smell our hands and breath, and thoroughly investigate the place after company left.

As for Christians, curiosity can also have its drawbacks. The world in which we live offers many allurements, and these can be destructive to our spiritual growth. John warned us, "Do not become attached to the world or the things in the world" (1 John 2:15). By world, John means the world system under which we live, not the earth itself. The world system is antagonistic to God, His people, plan, and program. The earth, on the other hand, is not our enemy but is here for our use and enjoyment. Paul tells us that creation itself yearns for the final redemption (Romans 8:18-22).

It is when the Christian takes his eyes off the Lord Jesus and become curious about the things in the world, forbidden fruit, if you will, that trouble begins. The desires of the old fallen nature, the cravings aroused by what is seen, and the

131

pride in acquiring possessions and pleasures are what John warns against when Christians start to get curious and stick their noses where they don't belong (1 John 2:16). Paul talks about believers going too far, getting in too deep, and making a "shipwreck" of the faith, that is, making a mockery of Christianity (1 Timothy 1:19).

The secret to overcoming an unhealthy curiosity is to cry out to the Lord for help, to dive into His Word for strength and wisdom, and to remember His loving sacrifice for all our sins and our salvation. If the problem is deep-seated psychologically, then perhaps professional counseling should be added to the above suggestions.

"Too soon old and too late smart!" So goes a saying attributed to the Pennsylvania Dutch. Unfortunately, it is all too true as we humans are often slow learners. We often lament, "If I knew then what I know now, things would be different." Part of the problem is our stubbornness, a reluctance to find a better way, to admit we may have been wrong, and an inner drive to be independent or our own boss. Like curiosity, stubbornness or independence can also be good and creative, but many times these characteristics are not beneficial.

To claim that cats are independent or stubborn is to say the sky is blue, or the grass is green. It is not a profound statement; everybody knows it. It seems to be a trait they possess that we will never change. Like curiosity, it can lead them into danger or even cause a frustrated person to mistreat them.

I have read one sad story after another about cats who were indoor/outdoor pets and were let out at night to "prowl" around the neighborhood. Their well-meaning owners thought they were doing their cats a favor, allowing them to exercise their "independence." Needless to say, these people lost their beloved felines to fates I would rather not discuss.

Taff and Tiff are not exceptions to the rule, although being pampered indoor pussycats has had its affect upon them and their independent spirit. They are used to being loved and fussed over and afforded a lot of attention. Tiffany has been molded into the more submissive of the two, but still reserves some independence for herself. Taffy, as I have stated before, is the "I'll do it my way on my time, thank you," little modern miss. She is resolved to maintain this legendary feline distinction no matter if it sometimes exasperates Brenda and me to no end. Taffy epitomizes the "I'll get back to you on that" attitude so often used to describe the independent cat. Unlike many felines, however, Taffy and Tiffany's well-being is not threatened by their independence or stubbornness.

Christians can become too independent and stubborn. Of course, God wants every individual to think for himself, to be creative, to get ahead, to be independent, Christians included. In America as in no other place, people have a great opportunity to realize their dreams and be successful and prosperous. Christians can rejoice in scriptures like Jeremiah 29:11 and Matthew 6:33 where God expresses His wish to bless them abundantly.

However, like cats, Christians can develop that "I'm my own boss, I don't need to be preached at or told what to do" attitude. Some even try to justify not attending and being involved in a local church. They claim they can get "closer" to God out in the woods or some other solitary place. While at Lancaster Bible College, I heard a visiting speaker refute this lame excuse with a cute statement: "Where does it say in Scripture that a Christian, or anyone for that matter, is to go out into a forest or remote area with a do-it-yourself-worship-kit?" The answer, of course, is it doesn't, but rather instructs believers to worship together every week (see Hebrews 10:25). Christians need fellowship, instruction, correction, encouragement, inspiration, communion, and love on a regular basis, and they can't get that by themselves somewhere out on a hillside.

Not all Christians go to the extreme of Demas, who, as Paul described, "Abandoned me, having fallen in love with this present era" (2 Timothy 4:9). The love and loyalty he should have had for the Lord Jesus, he showered upon the era in which he lived.

Christians can and do come to a place where they feel self-sufficient and the Lord's influence in their lives begins to wane. If they are confronted by other believers about their behavior, they often become defensive and stubborn. Anger and excuses become mechanisms to cover up guilt. How foolish to short-change themselves when the King of all the universe yearns to share His untold wealth with them.

When a Christian is "off doing his own thing," God suffers, too. He has endowed every believer with gifts and talents and abilities to serve Him in His Kingdom. If a Christian goes his own way and ignores God's rightful claim on his life, no doubt our patient heavenly Father will get someone else to do the task, but then the Christian settles for second best. No one can do quite the same job we as individuals are called by God to do. He has a plan for our lives and an agenda for us to follow, and He has equipped us to carry it out. The choice is ours.

Cats or Christians can be hurt by too much independence or self-sufficiency. Stubbornness does not help settle the problem either. Perhaps the best cure for Christians is found in our Lord's words to the church at Ephesus: "You have deserted your first love, have a change of mind and do the creative things you did at the beginning" (Revelation 2:4-5).

FEAR: Someone might say that this is a good characteristic for cats from a survival standpoint. With all the hazards outdoor cats face from automobiles to dogs to cat-haters, there is a lot to be said for their apprehension. However, it has many times worked in a bad way and led to injury or death for numerous terrified felines who did not know which way to turn. The poor animals can easily panic on a highway and instead of running to safety, run right into the path of an oncoming vehicle; others freeze in the presence of a vicious dog and do not climb a tree or leap to a high place; still others run into an open field in front of the sights of a gun-toting cat-killer. Reports from cat owners, animal organizations, and veterinarians all tell the sad stories of how cats, gripped with fear, ran *toward* danger rather than *away* from it.

Even indoor pets like ours are susceptible to injury or worse because of fear. I recall one incident some years ago when I went to pet Taffy, and it frightened her. She leaped into the air, spun around, and landed on a piece of paneling we had fastened to the door for protection against scratching. She was all right, of course, and after we examined her and calmed her down, I thought to myself, *from now on proceed with more caution.*

Another time I was holding Tiffany, and things were fine until Brenda came around the corner modeling one of her hats. Whether Tiff did not immediately recognize Brenda or was surprised by the hat, I do not know. In any event, she leaped from my arms and made a loud thump on the floor. She, too, was okay but we were becoming increasingly aware of why these little creatures are called "scaredy cats."

Again, horror stories abound of how frightened cats leap up on hot stove tops, hide in the bottom of a washer or dryer, dive through a window, are strangled or hung by extension cords, and so on. Our homes, unfortunately, provide many potential disasters when our feline friends become unsettled.

But what about Christians? They certainly should not be plagued by fear...should they? The answer, of course, is no, they should not be. However, the truth is that many are imprisoned by this paralyzing emotion that controls their thoughts and functions. They are intimidated by people, by animals, by news events, by the dark, by change, by aging, by God, and a host of other phobias. Psychologists' and psychiatrists' offices are filled with Christians caught in the grip of fear. Pick up a Bible concordance and notice how often the Word of God deals with the subject. True, many times the term "fear" is used in the sense of reverence and awe, but there are manifold instances in both the Old and New Testaments where it refers to old-fashioned fright. It truly is a "human" problem, Christians included.

God implores His people to trust in Him, to turn all their fears over to Him, and to allow Him to remove all their anxieties. Jesus lovingly counseled His disciples, "Do not even begin to allow your hearts to become agitated. You are trusting in God, so trust in Me as well" (John 14:1). Our Savior was telling them not to allow fear thoughts to get a foothold in their hearts and minds. He was assuring them that He had everything under control and could handle any problem a Christian could have, including fear. After all, His success rate was phenomenal.

In the scripture above, Jesus teaches His disciples to substitute faith for fear by simply trusting in Him to fill their troubled and frightened minds with His peace. "Peace I am leaving with you; My own peace I am giving to you," He told them (John 14:27). Fear is a very powerful force, but it cannot co-exist with faith, which is the mightiest force in the world. Fear cannot move mountains, but faith can (Matthew 17:20). So the answer to fear is faith—faith in Jesus, who is speaking for His Almighty Father, and who will give peace, assurance, and courage to all who ask Him (Mark 11:22-24).

Some Positive Characteristics

LOVING: If faith is the strongest force in the world, then love is a close second. I know that Paul said love is greater than faith and hope, and it is because without it faith and hope are meaningless. Faith and hope must be accompanied by love to be honored by God, to be worthwhile and effective (1 Corinthians 13:3,13).

But faith comes first; that is, one must exercise faith in Jesus to become a Christian. "And without faith it is impossible to appease God, because anyone who comes to Him must have faith that He exists, and that He is favorable to those who search for Him" (Hebrews 11:6). Once saving faith is placed in Jesus, then God's love is poured out into the believer's heart by the Holy Spirit, and that love is reciprocated to God and to others. A whole new level of living begins—a life on a higher plane, if you will—and it affects the mind, the emotions, and the will (see Romans 5:5). Faith in God makes real love possible.

Some people question whether or not animals are capable of expressing love. I once heard a man say that animals do not have personalities. His wife quickly corrected him, and I agreed with her. All I have to do is observe our two kitties to see the differences in them. We can do almost anything with Tiffany—she is so compliant. Not so Taffy! With her, we tread carefully and respect her touchy temperament. We wish she was more like her sister, but we love her and accept her as she is.

I firmly believe that animals are capable of loving and receiving love. I said it before that Brenda and I turned our two furballs into little lovebugs. They know that we love them and they love us, and they crave all the attention we can give them. Of course, we like our space and they like theirs, and it works out pretty well.

Two of our parishioners experienced the love of a loyal, dedicated pet first hand some years ago when quick action was imperative. Bob and Betty Jane Renn were enjoying an after-lunch snooze when all of a sudden Bob went into a seizure. He was relaxing in his recliner, and although he was shaking violently, he did not awaken Betty Jane, who was in a deep sleep just across the room in her chair. Sleeping on the floor between them was Lacy, their Golden Retriever, who had been a seeing-eye candidate.

The seizure did, however, awaken Lacy who sensed her master was in trouble. She went right to Betty Jane and woke her up the best way she knew how—by barking! When Betty

Jane awoke, Lacy ran over to Bob, and she saw what was happening. She immediately called 911 and within minutes the paramedics were there.

The ambulance crews, the hospital physicians, and nurses all attributed Bob's recovery to Lacy's quick action. She had been instrumental in saving his life. If we thought those two were close before, guess who became even closer pals? Lacy loved Bob and Betty Jane and proved it by acting quickly when they needed her the most. Needless to say, they will never forget this four-footed friend who became a lifesaver.

A less dramatic example of a loving pet trying to help its human happened in our home one fall. Brenda and I were watching an old movie entitled, *Imitation of Life*. If you have ever seen the film you know it is an emotional story with a sad ending. Both of us were misty eyed, but Brenda was a bit more affected than I was. Taffy had been sitting on our two-step stool near Brenda's recliner looking out the window. At the end of the movie, my wife leaned back in her chair trying to hold back some sobs but was failing miserably. Taffy had by now turned around and was watching Brenda intently, wondering what was wrong with her friend. When Brenda looked at her, Taffy stepped onto the arm of the chair with her two front feet and offered a paw toward her face. My loving partner could not help herself—she grabbed Taffy and hugged and kissed her. More misty eyes! And, a thank you to the good Lord who gave us another lesson in something we take too often for granted— love.

We all, I'm sure, have read true stories in which loving pets saved their master's lives and often at the expense of their own. How many dogs and cats held a vigil at their master's grave or waited near their favorite chair? I remember a television account of a Siamese cat who drove its master's murderer to confess to the crime. It was eerie to see how this cunning little feline did not rest until its adversary was brought to justice. The cat eluded family members who wanted to take her home; she evaded the police who tried to catch her a few times; she got away from neighbors; and most importantly, she eluded the murderer who tried to kill her. I think that a patient police detective, who became suspicious, brought the murderer in. After the cat was finished with him, he was only too ready to confess. When its mission was accomplished, the kitty "turned itself in" to a member of the family and was given a good home and treated like royalty. If I remember correctly, the family took the cat to its master's home periodically to visit, and they did not sell the house for some time afterwards.

Was it love that drove this little creature to bring about the apprehension of the person who killed its master? The victim's family thought so as they recalled the close relationship the two had and how the cat seemed to never forget its former master. I am sure that many would dispute that claim, but I agree with the family. An animal is capable of love and will often go to great lengths to prove it.

Of all people, Christians should be "experts" in love. Jesus told His disciples, "Show love for one another. Just as I have loved you, so you must show love for one another. By this, all people will come to know that you are my disciples, if you show love to each other" (John 13:34-35).

The Apostle Paul describes the love our Lord is speaking of in 1 Corinthians 13 as a love of intelligent comprehension and corresponding purpose. In other words, it sees a need and takes appropriate action to fill it. The Greek word used of God's love and Christian love is *agape*, and it denotes a higher form of affection than the other term *phileo*, which is often translated "fond of" or "friendship." This love in action on the part of God is best illustrated in the famous verse John 3:16, "For God so greatly loved the world that He gave up His only unique Son, so that whoever believes in Him will not perish but have everlasting life."

On the part of Christians, this love may be best expressed by what Jesus said in John 15:12-13: "Show love to one another

139

as I have demonstrated My love to you. No greater love has anyone than this, that he should lay down his life for his friends." In these two verses we find what I continually tell my people about this love: It is supernatural, unconditional, and sacrificial. Is this not an accurate description of what Jesus did for all of us on the cross? He supernaturally, unconditionally, and sacrificially laid down His perfect life not only for His friends, but for His enemies, too. The people of the world are not generally known for demonstrating this kind of love, but Christians should be. It is a love that cannot be produced by human effort, no matter how sincere. It is Jesus loving people through His redeemed believers who yield to His influence and will. It is a love that is desperately needed by a lost and hurting world.

As I said earlier, "Let the animals teach you" was wise advice from Job. Over the years, we have learned so much from them, just by observation, lessons which should make us better and nobler. God acknowledges this in Isaiah 43:20 when He says, "The untamed animals pay honor to Me." Animals outdoing humans in honoring God? Unfortunately, yes, many times they do. One area we urgently need their instruction in is this thing called love.

Think about it! They do not care if we are good looking or homely, thin or heavy, tall or short, rich or poor, black or white, red or yellow. They just love us! No strings attached! No prejudice, no bigotry, no matter! They give us their love, unadulterated and true. Oh, how we need to be like that!

LOYALTY: Siamese are perhaps better known than any other breed for being one-person cats. I found this to be true with my own Siamese to some extent and with other pets I have known. Tiffany #1 was a loyal cat and was ready to defend me on several occasions. When some of my college buddies and I were horsin' around, Tiffany positioned herself between us, growling and hissing at the other students. My boxer dog had done something similar when my neighborhood chums and I roughhoused with each other, but this was unusual, at least for me, to see a cat protect its master. Normally, we would expect a cat to run under something when it senses trouble.

Taffy seems to be another exception. Of course, things like thunder, motorcycles, loud cars and trucks, sirens, or any other unexpected noise will scare her and send her scurrying for cover. However, one time some years ago, I began tickling Brenda on the bed, and she cried out in a high-pitched shrill voice, "Taffy, Taffy...help, help, Mommy needs you," several times. Within a flash I had a multi-colored cat on the bed staring me in the face with a very serious expression as if to say, "You better not be hurting her!" We repeated this afterward with much the same result, although I think that Taffy was beginning to catch on to our ruse. On a couple of occasions, Tiffany followed her sister to see what was going on but probably more out of curiosity than any rescue inclinations. She didn't seem too convinced that Brenda was in any danger.

Like other animals, cats will defend their young even against much larger adversaries. I have heard of almost human-like incidents of loyalty on the part of cats to their kittens and to their masters. Witness the mother cat of some years ago who braved fire to rescue her little ones from a burning building. She was burned badly herself, but this loyal feline got them all out and received national attention.

I have read of cats who fended off would-be intruders, stayed by an injured child or adult or went for help, of cats who like guardian angels protected the ones they loved with a loyalty that would not die. We cat lovers love to read these accounts or hear of them, and I know one preacher who has been known to use them in sermon illustrations. (Don't bother asking, I won't reveal his name!)

Loyalty is another positive feature of God's people. Inspiring stories abound of Christians over the centuries who have exhibited unearthly loyalty to Jesus at an expense many would not be willing to pay. They were willing to risk everything for Him because their faith was real. The list of Christian martyrs is a long one.

We must insert here that loyalty should not be confused with or misunderstood for fanaticism. The willingness to lay down one's life for Jesus rather than deny Him does not indicate a distorted view or value of life, but a loving devotion to the living God who gives life. Terrorists and other misguided "religious" fanatics who destroy themselves and other people in the name of God have no real concept of the meaning and value of life. A mentally healthy Christian will not commit suicide or take the life of another human being. Both acts are foreign to the new nature we receive from God. Both are forbidden by God's Word, which teaches a high and holy value of life. Loyalty to God the Father and His Son Jesus Christ is a dedication that is sane and sensible because there is a realization that life here is a testing ground for the life to come. Christian loyalty is inspired by faith and love and the worthiness of the One to whom it is given.

In the Old Testament economy, David prayed, "I am aware, my God, that You examine the heart and are delighted with integrity. And I have observed with joy how willingly Your people who are presented here have given to You. O Lord...keep this yearning in the hearts of Your people forever, and keep their hearts loyal to You" (1 Corinthians 29: 17-18).

In the New Testament, Paul wrote to the Roman Christians, "So then, I am appealing to you now, Brothers, in view of the compassionate expressions of God, to make a complete presentation of your bodies as a sacrifice, yet living, holy, one acceptable to God, which is your reasonable, sacred service" (Romans 12:1). The Apostle reminds us of our sacred obligation to God—our duty to be loyal to Him. He says that it is our reasonable or logical responsibility in light of all He has done for us. Serious believers have no trouble accepting this responsibility to obey and follow Jesus as Savior and Master, knowing the magnanimous impact He has had upon their lives!

We covet the love and loyalty of our cats and are glad when they give us undeniable demonstrations of their devotion to us. Our heavenly Father desires the loyalty of His people as well and is pleased when we think enough of Him to express it in our lives. We may never be called upon to lay down our lives for Him, but He is happy to know that we would be willing. The Christian's loyalty is well-placed. It is a high, holy, and noble dedication that cannot be matched. If our kitties are any inspiration, then let their loyalty to us remind us of ours to Him.

PATIENCE: If you ever watched a cat on a hunt stalking its prey, then you know that our feline friends are very patient creatures. They will crouch or sit for long periods of time watching the object of their fascination. It may be the proverbial mouse, a bird, a mole, a chipmunk, or even an insect of some sort. It makes no difference; they will position themselves and wait for the right moment to strike. Time is of no essence to the cat—it has all day! To this able little hunter, the prize is worth the wait.

The fact that cats have been brought indoors usually does not change them. In a previous chapter I described how Taffy and Tiffy set up "stake-outs" in various places of the house, especially in front of the French doors in the living and dining rooms. They spend a couple of hours watching the openings in those doors. And, as I stated before, Tiffany apprehended two mice and brought them to us, so the patience paid off.

This little squirt will also sit patiently for long periods of time if you let her, waiting for an invite up on your lap. She approaches, looking up at you with an inquiring meow or a sound faintly resembling a meow. This is to signal to you that she is there and is asking permission to come aboard. Tiff is very adept at staring you down, and she applies this technique with amazing results. After all, how can you resist this little gray and white ball of fur with the cute face and big dark eyes who loves you and wants to be with you? She is very proficient at laying a guilt trip on you if you do not, at that time, wish to be bothered. I must confess that more often than not Brenda and I give in.

The outdoor cats we came to know over the years, beginning with Candy, the original "parsonage cat," were for the most part good, patient hunters. Candy was very street smart, too, and lived a long, prolific life. Tyco, our cats' mother, was also a patient hunter and was very successful in bringing back various kinds of prey. Coco, Tyco's sister, also comes to mind as an able, patient stalker who always brought back the goods.

One of the fruits of the Holy Spirit is patience as Paul tells us in Galatians 5:22, and it is a very important virtue for the Christian to possess. We do not live in a slow, laid-back society like the European or Eastern countries, or even Mexico, for that matter. Our lifestyle here in America is fast-paced—rush here and there, instant this and that, get it done now, heart attack city. No wonder some wise individual once described Christians as praying, "Lord, give me patience…and I want it now!" This seems especially true of American Christians who have been caught up in the jet-set pace like everyone else. We want answers to our prayers, and we want them now! However, God is not tied to space and time, and He is definitely not on our time schedule.

We need to develop patience as children of God and learn to wait and not run ahead of Him. It's when we get ahead of Him that we encounter trouble and often make a mess of things. Then we go back to the Lord asking Him to get us out of it. Because He loves us, He does just that.

There are various Greek words in the New Testament translated "patience" and my favorite is the term *hupomene*. It is a combination of two words *hupo* meaning "under," and *mene* meaning "to remain." Thus the word means "to remain under." It is an apt description of Christian patience or endurance!

Many times, God asks us to "remain under," that is, bear up under a burden or the pressure of some problem or difficulty. It isn't pleasant at the time, but He knows what He is doing, and we will benefit from the learning process. Paul tells us that we should not shrink away from suffering, troubles, or trials, because when we bear up under them we become stronger and better people (see Romans 5:3.5). God does not cause suffering or problems, but He allows them to come into our lives for a purpose. He asks us to be patient, to wait, and to trust. For a great example of patience, read the Old Testament book of Job.

Cats are naturally patient, and we Christians need to become that way. So let's allow the Holy Spirit to cultivate this wonderful virtue within us for our benefit, the benefit of other people, and for the benefit of God's kingdom.

ADAPTABILITY: After Sammy's death, our neighbor Bill's brother Mark and his wife Barbara brought a coal-black kitten to ease the pain of losing that special little feline friend. She reminded us of Sammy right away, having a lot of the same personality traits and being almost a dead-ringer for her predecessor.

I wanted to name her Sammy II, but Louise began calling her "Stinky" because the little stinkpot kept getting into dangerous situations. She followed us across the road, went into the barnyard with the cattle, and got into other potentially hazardous positions. Hence the name "Stinky" stuck!

Her carefree, fearless demeanor cost her that autumn when she ventured into the field with Bill's Black Angus cattle. Barb and Brenda had husked some corn and threw the husks to the cows. The cats followed along thinking that there might be something in it for them, Stinky included. Everyone got out unscathed except Stinky, who apparently was stepped on by one of the cows. Her left front leg was injured beyond repair and curled up into a permanent hook shape. Barb, Louise, and

Brenda all nursed her with cleansing lotions and healing ointments, and the little tyke survived although now as a three-
legged cat.

Stinky had, up to that time, received preferential treatment
from all of us, but after her injury that intensified greatly.
When leftovers were given as treats, the tri-foot kitty was given
the best of the food, and the other cats were kept at bay while
she ate. This was quite a feat sometimes because Stinky was a
slow eater. I wondered if it was necessary because her injury
did not seem to diminish her spirit. Stinky certainly did not
get "pushed around."

When we would call her, she would come running on her
three legs, and the other cats did not leave her behind. Brenda
fed her on top of a tool chest I made her out of tongue and
groove wood. Little Stinky had no trouble leaping up on top.
She would just give herself a little more thrust from her back
legs it seemed, knowing that she had one good front leg with
which to catch herself once on top. After she first was injured,
we picked her up and put her up on the tool chest, but as she
adapted herself to her handicap, she did not give us time to
pick her up—she jumped up herself, surprising us. Like
Sammy, little Stinky had been an inspiration to us all. With
neurological problems developing in my right hand and arm,
causing me to guide and steady it with my left hand in order to
write legibly, I often looked at Stinky and thanked the Lord
that I have a right hand.

Many stories abound about cats and other animals that
adapted to physical handicaps of some sort, and there are incidents in which animals had to adapt where there were no
physical problems. Such is the case of a cat and a bantam
rooster who lived on my sister and brother-in-law's farm some
years ago. Nancy and Elwood were not "farmers" in the full
sense of the word, but they purchased a 52 acre farm some
time ago and had some farm animals, including cats and
chickens. They also had some fine horses, one of which was a

stately Tennessee Walker that was Elwood's. Both of them worked full-time jobs and enjoyed toying with the farm almost as a hobby.

For whatever reason, the cat and the rooster were outcasts on the farm. The other barn cats rejected their feline counterpart and would not allow him to mingle with the group. He had many battle scars to prove it. The situation was similar for the bantam rooster. He had scars and missing feathers to show his rejection. However, the two teamed up and defended one another against the other cats and roosters. It was a real "odd couple."

Since they could not eat with their own kind, they ate together and for the most part they "ate out." By that I mean they trekked up the short distance to my parents' home and rummaged in the compost out back. (Mom and Dad had purchased over an acre from Nancy and Elwood and had a nice corner property on the edge of the farm.)

Mom had told me about these two ostracized outcasts over the phone, and I made sure I had my camera the next vacation we took to Beech Creek. I was not disappointed. One morning after breakfast, Mom looked out the window down towards Nancy's and, lo and behold, the two rejects were making their way up through the yard on their way to the compost behind the house.

I watched them as they walked slowly side by side, apparently in no hurry, to feast together at the compost. Brenda and I were amazed at the sight and even more at how they seemed to communicate with each other. Talk about a universal language! These two, so completely different, had broken all barriers down and had formed a friendship. There they were—two natural enemies to a degree—a cat and a bird, but they forgot about their differences or didn't know it, or didn't care. It was wonderful to watch, and I thank God for the opportunity and the privilege of seeing this unusual bond for myself.

And what about us? Why can't we forget about race, color,

and differences? Why can't we humans worldwide be willing to form unlikely, unheard of alliances and help each other? Why can't we be like the cat and the rooster who didn't seem to have a problem with being friends and being nice to each other?

Someone may say that the the cat and the rooster became a duo out of necessity in order to survive, and that if they had not been rejected by their own species, this alliance would have not been formed. Maybe...and maybe not! No one really knows, do they? Stranger things have happened. In any event, we can learn from their friendship, necessary or not, and lay aside our prejudices and preconceived ideas. As Job said, "But inquire of the animals, and they will instruct you."

Like Stinky who adapted to her physical malady, these two little critters adapted to their social situation, if I may call it that. It goes to show that God has built into all His creatures, great and small, the ability to adapt or adjust to unfavorable conditions if they will look around and utilize those abilities. When you find yourself in a situation similar to the cat and the rooster, what do you do? No doubt the same thing they did— find a friend. It really doesn't matter that the friend isn't exactly like you as long as he accepts you. Acceptance is the important thing. Everyone needs it!

Can anyone adapt better than a Christian? Is anyone existing in more unfavorable conditions than the child of God? Is anyone trying to function in a more adverse state than a follower of Jesus Christ? The Savior Himself put it in no uncertain terms, "Since this world hates you, remember that it hated Me first" (John 15:18). It is true that at this present time believers in other countries are experiencing more persecution than Christians here in America. Horror stories abound of mistreatment, torture, imprisonment, and even murder. But beware, there are antagonistic forces in this nation that would like nothing better than to still the voice of Christianity.

Christians all over America should be alert and aware of

the threats to their religious freedoms because they are out there. People working against Christians have infiltrated every arena: government, business, the media, medicine, education, and even religion itself. The Christian's enemy takes on many forms. No wonder, because the one who empowers them is able to present himself as "an angel of light" (2 Corinthians 11:14). Satan is behind much of the evil we see in this world, and he inspires and encourages all who are willing to do his bidding.

The Christian has to adapt to the conditions he finds in the society in which he lives without compromising his faith. He wants to be accepted as an individual who happens to be a disciple of Jesus Christ, and he wants to display the positive, healthy ideals and principles of his Savior. He does not want to come off as a fanatic or a kook, he does not think that he has the only corner on God's truth, and he does not think that he is better than others who may disagree with him. He does believe his way, or rather the Christian way, is the best and the only way and for good reason. Then Jesus said, "I am the way and the truth and the life. No one can come to the Father except through Me" (John 14:6).

So the Christian has to adapt to living in a hostile environment where he resides as an alien, "For they are not of this world as I am not of this world" (John 17:14). It takes wisdom and savvy to be successful and influential in this unfriendly-to-Christians world, and it covers every area of life.

First, there is his personal life in which he must be all right with himself, and with his Lord. Self-acceptance and self-love are important and vital to personal growth. The Christian needs to see himself as a child of God with divinely imparted gifts, talents, and abilities. He needs to see himself as God does, a valuable asset to this world and His kingdom. And he needs to maintain a close, spiritual relationship with God through prayer, Bible study and reading, regular personal devotions, regular church worship, and fellowship with other Christians. He must be comfortable here in order to move on to the next area.

If the believer is not all right with himself, and with God, it will be difficult for him to relate well to another person. He must understand that he is to present himself as an integrated, well-rounded, loving individual to hurting, searching, and sometimes antagonistic and skeptical people. That's a tall order, and the Christian must have all his ducks in a row to be able to do it. If he is to be successful in helping others to come to God through Jesus, he must come across as a happy, satisfied disciple of the Man from Galilee.

Then there is his family life. Some Christians have the idea that they do not have to give their families the same consideration they give to other people. That is contrary to Scripture which commands respect and loving consideration to everyone, especially family members and fellow believers. Compare Ephesians 5:21-33, Galatians 6:10, and 1 Thessalonians 4:11-12. The Christian family is to be a shining model to those outside the fold of God, a model that attracts people to desire the love, the warmth, and the joy the children of the Lord have without measure.

Having described what the Christian should be and what he is up against in this world, I believe it is necessary to explain that all of this relates to normal people with ordinary problems. The Bible basically is written to normal individuals who can understand and apply its positive principles with some difficulty but also with great success. Yes, the principles require supernatural spiritual assistance—the indwelling Holy Spirit—and the Christian who relies upon His wisdom, guidance, and strength will be able to adapt to His leading and instruction. See Ephesians 5:18 and Galatians 5:16-26.

A Christian who has a psychosis or some other mental or emotional disorder may require professional help in applying the therapeutic principles of God's Word. It may be difficult and time consuming, but it can be done and it is well worth it. Too often such believers do not receive the help they need or deserve, the help God wants them to have. The help is there, it is available, and there are capable, understanding, and compassionate trained counselors ready to work with people to overcome their serious problems.

Normal, well-adjusted Christians are able to adapt to change or adverse situations better than those who do not know Jesus as Savior. They are conditioned by their faith to respond, not to react, to whatever strange or difficult state they find themselves in. Paul expressed this ability when he wrote, "I have learned to be content in whatever situation I am" (Philippians 4:12). With God's help, any trusting Christian who wishes to honor his Lord and Master can do the same.

Cats and Christians are great adapters. God has made them so. Whether it is little Stinky with the bum leg, or the cat-rooster combination, or the blind leper who had to read his Braille Bible with his tongue, or the Christian paralytic who wrote a best-seller with a tape recorder, we can be encouraged or inspired by cats and Christians who have much in common.

"But Inquire of the Animals, and They Will Instruct You."

Job's words are well taken. There is much to be learned in observing animals, and cats in particular. Cat lovers are very much aware of this and are amazed at how they can learn something new from their feline friends on a regular basis. The secret is to be alert and sensitive to these amazing creatures our loving God has blessed us with.

I have heard many people relate how their cat taught them to live and to love again. There are also multitudes of stories of how dogs have done the same thing. I am not surprised, for they are God's creatures, too. Our wise and loving Creator has put all things here on earth for a purpose, and that purpose always involves us. Let's realize one thing despite all the propaganda to the contrary: God loves us and has our best interests at heart. He proved that 2000 years ago when He sent His Son to die on the cross for our sins. Read John 3:16, Ephesians 5:1-2, and Philippians 2:5-8.

In our case, with Taffy and Tiffany, we have seen how these two little furballs come to us and soothe our troubled spirits after a trying day. They just come, unassuming, accepting, loving. They make us forget the problems and pressures of the day and ease our cluttered and confused mental state with their companionship. There is something therapeutic about a purring cat who just wants to be with you and love you with no strings attached. My Aunt Ann, who has been a widow for over half a century, does not know what she would do without her feline friend. Like many of us cat lovers, Aunt Ann understands how caring for a pet helps her in her need to give love and, of course, to receive love from her adoring kitty.

Retirement centers, nursing homes, and apartment complexes for senior citizens have all seen the value of allowing pets for their residents. Some nursing homes do it on a visiting basis. The presence of a pet perks people up and brings joy into an otherwise uneventful day. When an elderly person gets a pet, they have a new reason to live and the pet enjoys giving them affection.

Cats seem to be the better choice when it comes to a pet for elderly people. Other than the convenience of not having to let them out several times a day, cats are less demanding than dogs. Man's best friend often wants attention all the time and may pester his master to play or go for a walk, depending on the age of the dog. Of course, it also depends on the disposition of the elderly person. Such a pet may be just what the doctor ordered. Cats, however, are independent and are willing to spend some time alone or at least give "their person" time to rest or relax. They present a challenge sometimes, especially if their master wants to shower them with affection, and they retreat somewhere seeking a little solitude. Once again, it's up to the individual whether a cat or dog is best.

As a minister, I preach, teach, and counsel people to become the wonderful, creative individuals God created them to be. The Bible is the best "self-help" book on the market and has been called "God's Love Letter to the World." It encourages us to know ourselves with our strengths and weaknesses (Proverbs 1:1-2), to accept ourselves as unique children of God with purpose and meaning (Proverbs 2:1-6), to regulate and discipline ourselves for positive and beneficial living (Proverbs 1:3; 3:5-6), to share ourselves with others in acts of love and benevolence (Proverbs 3:27), and as Christians, to show others the way to God (Proverbs 11:30), and much, much more. I encourage the reader to delve into the Bible and find in this amazing, supernaturally written book the answers not only to life's problems but to life itself. There are many good versions available with appropriate helps.

So what does this have to do with cats who are not even mentioned in the Bible (other than the lion and the leopard)? Just this: Cats can help us to know ourselves as we observe their personalities and take note of how they handle the pressures of life. They can help us accept ourselves as we watch them unconditionally accept us as we are. They can help us discipline ourselves and regulate our lives more efficiently as we observe their routines and orderly habits. They can help us learn to share ourselves with others as they share themselves with us and draw us out of our seclusiveness with their winsome ways. I believe that they can also show us the way to God if we let them by their loving, accepting, and forgiving characteristics. All of God's creation calls out to honor Him as the Psalmist wrote, "The universe declares the glory of God" (Psalm 19:1). We can see the Creator in everything that He has made if we are sincere, open, and observant. Even our little feline friends can tell us some things about God.

"Christians are like cats." I think at least Christian cat-lovers will agree. We certainly appreciate their high intelligence and the Christian-like characteristics they manifest. We are happy that they teach people to live and to love again. (And isn't that what Christians are supposed to do?) God bless the kitties and let's take a lesson from them. "But inquire of the animals and they will instruct you."

Chapter 14

A Final Word

We have learned a lot over the years from Taffy and Tiffany and the outdoor cats that have touched our lives in some way. We have been blessed to have "met" Candy, Smokey, Charcoal, Tyco, Coco, Tigger, and, of course, Sammy and Stinky. They all have shown us unconditional love, something we humans need to be reminded of time after time. We are so easily hurt or offended, and we almost enjoy nurturing a grudge or refusing to forgive and forget. Although it is true that such actions on our part are detrimental to our health, it is equally true that such conduct is wrong. Paul told us in Colossians 3:13, "Be patient with one another and be willing to forgive whatever disagreements you have accumulated against each other. Be willing to forgive as the Lord forgave you."

Yes, cats have excellent memories, and they make mental notes of those people who mistreat them. They often have squabbles among themselves but nearly always seem to reach an understanding in order to keep peace and survive. Taff and Tiff do their share of growling, hissing, and swatting—remember the big cat spat—but eventually they are washing each other or sleeping together. They seem to be willing to overlook each other's infractions and ours, too. How different our lives would be if we followed their example. Isn't this what our Jesus implored us to do? "But I am telling you, show love to your adversaries and pray for those who mistreat you" (Matthew 5:44). Our Savior knows that we need to develop a functional harmony, for our own welfare and for everyone else.

Our feline friends have also taught us something about attitude; that is, a general overall attitude toward life. Attitudes often determine actions, and if our outlook on life is not positive and healthy, then our lives can be miserable. An optimistic or hopeful view of life helps us get through the troubles and trials of living in a pressure-cooker society. God never promised us a rose garden or an easy-street way of living, but rather told us up front that things could get rough. "In this world you will have problems" (John 16:33). The secret is not to try to avoid trouble, conflict, and suffering, but instead face it with a positive, "all things are possible" attitude. Jesus said, "But be optimistic, I overcame the world!" (John 16:33). Since He overcame the world with all its temptations, trials, and perils, then so can we with His help and guidance. Paul told us, "You should develop the same attitude as that of Christ Jesus" (Philippians 2:5). Things will be much better for us if we do.

I remember little beloved Sammy who loved life and feared nothing. She thought everyone, human and animal alike, was her friend...and is that totally wrong? She displayed a happy-go-lucky attitude which was contagious, and we were affected by this little joyful, frolicking feline. I again affirm that God sent her into our lives.

Our own Tiffany has shown us both qualities: unconditional love and a positive attitude or outlook on life. Tiff basically is a carefree, fun-loving, happy "catster"! She is a lovebug who just can't give enough love without really expecting anything in return. She follows us around wanting to be with us and showering us with affection. This little gray and white kitty seems to refuse to have a bad day. Her face radiates happiness, and I often think that she is smiling, especially when she is drooling in ecstasy. Her bright eyes shine with sheer joy, and she just seems so happy to be alive.

One of Tiffany's nicknames is Kamikaze Cat which, if you remember, we gave her because she seems so accident prone. As I stated before, everything we throw to her seems to be drawn to her head like a magnet. At playtime we were tempted to equip her with a hard hat or some sort of helmet. However, Tiff is determined, and after being "bonked" on the bean or "roughed up" in a wrasslin' match with Mommy or Daddy or Taffy, she is right back for more. After a few of these exasperating experiences, Brenda remarked, "Tiffany is like Timex: She takes a licking and keeps on ticking." Nothing deters this little gray and white ball of fur from her appointed rounds of spreading joy and goodwill throughout the parsonage. She has chosen to be happy, to overlook the bad things in life and overcome them with good, and to give herself unconditionally even if it hurts. Hmmm! Didn't Someone else we know do that about 2000 years ago? Critics to the contrary, it's the best way—no, it's the only way to live.

We all have choices, and the choices we make can affect us and others in very serious ways. If we make wrong choices, we will have to live with them and perhaps suffer some consequences. Even right choices can cause us pain, but at least we will have the satisfaction of knowing we chose the proper course of action. It all comes down to responsibility, something many people want to avoid or evade these days. God help us to make right choices.

So, "Inquire of the animals, and they will instruct you" (Job 12:7). Let your cat, your dog, your hamster, your parrot, your pig, your pet, teach you what life is all about. Let them fulfill their most important mission of this earth: to direct you to the Creator who loves you so much that He gave His only Son for you. God bless you and your wonderful pet.

TAFFY AND TIFFANY

Two "squirts" who know how to elicit the love and care that make them feel special—that's our two little ones. They have had more adventures than could fill just one book! Somehow they keep finding new challenges and overcoming them in the most unlikely ways!

There was the time recently when...but that will have to wait for another book. Right now, watch your own cat carefully and ask some friends about theirs. I bet you'll be surprised to discover just what interesting scrapes all cats seem to get themselves into. You may even learn one of life's little lessons along the way. Remember our favorite verse: "Ask the animals and they will teach you" (Job 12:7).

—Clair & Brenda Shaffer

Clair Shaffer was born and raised in rural, central Pennsylvania. While working his way through college, he raised a cat and began to appreciate all her quirks and delights. He had a wide variety of work experiences and enjoyed being a manager of personnel for a retail store where he worked with his wife Brenda for three years before they were married. About 16 years ago, he took a temporary position as a pastor of two churches and has been with them ever since. He currently is working on his doctorate degree.

Clair has loved writing all his life, having kept a sports notebook containing game details and stats of the local team from the last 45 years. After reading numerous cat books, he decided that his cats, Taffy and Tiffany, lived as exciting a life of any he had read about and began to put their lively escapades down on paper.

This book is an account of the adventures they have had with their two feline companions and is filled with life's little lessons, sprinkled liberally with humor.